WRITTEN IN LIGHT

WRITTEN IN LIGHT

Antonio Garrido Caballero

CONTENTS

The Weight of Silence

The morning bell tolled through the convent, rolling over the hills like a soft ripple across water. Stone walls, kissed by the dawn's pale light, seemed to hum with the vibration, welcoming another day. Inside, the sisters stirred, a rustle of habits and hushed whispers echoing through the narrow hallways. The faint shuffle of feet on stone floors and the soft clink of pots in the kitchen gave the air a kind of rhythm, marking the beginning of another day in their routine.

Lucía was already awake, sitting on the edge of her narrow cot, her legs crossed beneath her. The convent's single small window framed her in light, golden beams catching on her dark hair, which hung loose and wild around her face. Her fingers hovered over a worn leather notebook, the one she carried everywhere, the one no one else was allowed to touch. Its corners were frayed, its spine cracked from years of use, and the faint smell of ink lingered on its pages like a shadow.

From below, the faint sound of Sister Beatriz scolding someone rose through the air, sharp and clipped. Lucía tilted her head, listening with a smile that played at the corners of her lips.

"I said water them gently! Not drown them! Are we raising roses or seaweed, Sister Patricia?" Beatriz's exasperation pierced through the calm of the morning.

"I'm doing my best, Sister Beatriz! They looked thirsty!" Patricia's defensive tone made Lucía stifle a laugh.

Lucía pressed the notebook tightly against her chest for a moment, her face contemplative. The leather felt warm against her skin, as though it had absorbed her secrets, her prayers, her confessions. Then she opened it, her pen poised with deliberation. She hesitated, her fingers trembling slightly, before scrawling words across the page in her precise, flowing script.

"Today," she wrote, each letter taking shape slowly, deliberately. *"Today, I will not use it."*

But even as she wrote the words, a faint hum, like the first note of a hymn, pulsed through her fingertips. The pen felt alive in her hand, and a strange sensation ran up her arm—a warmth, a pull, a whisper of something that begged to be released. She stared at the ink, which seemed to shimmer for a brief moment before settling into the page.

The creak of the door startled her. Lucía turned to find Sister Isabel leaning against the frame, her plump face twisted into a familiar mix of exasperation and affection. Isabel's habit was slightly askew, and her hair, always refusing to stay tucked under her veil, curled rebelliously around her temples.

"Skipping breakfast again, are you?" Isabel said, her eyebrow raised in a mock challenge. She leaned against the doorframe, arms crossed, her eyes drifting inevitably to the notebook in Lucía's lap.

Lucía quickly flipped it shut and shook her head, but her cheeks betrayed her, flushing a soft pink.

"Mmhmm," Isabel said knowingly, stepping into the room and sitting down on the cot beside her. "Let me guess. Another earth-shattering revelation? Or are you writing my biography now? If you are, please don't leave out the time I managed to sneak chocolate into Lent. That was a masterpiece of divine rebellion."

Lucía rolled her eyes, her lips curling into a silent laugh. Her pen scratched across the page quickly, and she held the notebook up to Isabel.

"It's private."

"Private, huh?" Isabel tilted her head, squinting at the letters as if trying to decode them. Isabel chuckled, her eyes narrowing playfully. "You know, one day you're going to write something that changes everything. And when you do, don't forget who gave you the inspiration!". And by the way, don't forget to mention my unmatched skill at burning toast. It's practically a miracle in itself."

Lucía couldn't suppress the silent laughter bubbling up, her shoulders shaking. She wrote again, her strokes bold and quick.

"You're impossible."

"And you're predictable," Isabel shot back, her teasing tone softening as her gaze lingered on Lucía's face. She reached out, resting a hand on Lucía's shoulder. "You know we worry about you, don't you? Always tucked away with that book of yours. God made us a community for a reason, Lucía. Don't keep yourself so apart."

Lucía paused, her hand hovering over the notebook, her smile fading slightly. She stared at Isabel for a moment, then nodded, her expression soft but resolute. She wrote again, her pen moving with care.

"I'm fine. Truly."

"Truly?" Isabel squinted at, leaning closer with mock suspicion. "That's the best you've got? Truly? That's as convincing as Sister Beatriz claiming she loves everyone equally when we know she'd trade all of us for a well-pruned rosebush."

Lucía's grin returned, her shoulders shaking again with laughter. She flipped the notebook closed and tucked it under her arm, the gesture protective but not defensive.

"Fine, fine," Isabel said, throwing up her hands in exaggerated surrender. "I'll leave you to your mysteries. But at least come outside with me. The roses look terrible, and I swear if I have to listen to Beatriz rant one more time, I'll need divine intervention."

Lucía tilted her head, intrigued. The roses were her favorite, and the thought of them drooping in the morning sun made her stomach twist slightly. She stood, sliding off the cot with ease, and gestured for Isabel to lead the way.

As they walked down the stone corridor, the morning light filtered through the stained-glass windows, casting fragmented rainbows across the walls. Isabel's chatter filled the air, her voice a mix of teasing and genuine warmth.

"You know," Isabel began, "the other sisters are starting to take bets on what's inside that notebook of yours."

Lucía glanced at her, raising an eyebrow.

"I'm serious!" Isabel continued, her tone animated. "Sister Patricia thinks you're writing recipes. Beatriz swears it's a list of sins—which, let's be honest, means hers is probably the longest."

Lucía shook her head, smiling.

"But me?" Isabel leaned closer, her voice dropping to a conspiratorial whisper. "I think it's poetry. Romantic poetry. About that carpenter who delivered the new pews last month. What was his name again? Miguel? Oh, the way he smiled at you, Lucía. If you weren't so busy scribbling, you might've noticed."

Lucía stopped mid-step, her cheeks flaming red. She whirled on Isabel, her eyes wide with indignation as she scribbled furiously in her notebook. She shoved it at Isabel, her face alight with silent fury.

"You're impossible!"

Isabel burst out laughing, throwing her arm around Lucía's shoulders as they stepped into the garden. "There she is. That's the fire I've been looking for. Come on, mute poet. Let's see if we can save Beatriz's precious roses before she declares them martyrs."

The garden was alive with the scents of earth and flowers, the air thick with the buzz of bees. Sister Beatriz was crouched over a bush, muttering darkly as she inspected the leaves.

"Look at this," Beatriz said, waving a drooping stem in their direction. "Neglect. Pure, unholy neglect. These poor roses deserve better than this."

Lucía knelt beside the bush, her fingers brushing lightly over the petals. She frowned, pulling out her notebook.

"What's she doing now?" Beatriz asked Isabel, her voice tinged with suspicion.

"Saving the day," Isabel replied breezily, plopping onto a nearby bench.

Lucía wrote quickly, her pen moving with determination. She turned the notebook toward Beatriz, who squinted at the words.

"They need shade in the afternoon. The sun is too harsh."

Beatriz straightened, her lips pursed in thought. "Hmph. Makes sense. Didn't think of that. Maybe you should be the one in charge of the garden."

Lucía shook her head, her smile soft as she reached for her pen again.

"I'm better with words than plants."

"Ha!" Isabel laughed from the bench. "That's the understatement of the year."

Lucía glanced at her, rolling her eyes but unable to suppress her grin. The three of them fell into a rhythm—Beatriz muttering instructions, Isabel providing a running commentary, and Lucía quietly, diligently tending to the roses.

For a brief moment, the world felt whole, simple, and untouched by the complexities of Lucía's gift. But deep down, she knew it couldn't stay that way.

The garden was alive with sound: the chirp of birds, the buzz of bees flitting between the herbs, and the steady murmur of sisters working. Lucía knelt near the rosebushes, her fingers tracing the edges of their wilting petals. The vibrant reds and yellows she loved were muted, tinged with brown, as though the life had seeped out of them overnight.

Beatriz bustled over, her expression sharp. "I told Mother Superior these roses needed pruning weeks ago," she huffed, shaking her head. "Now look at them. They're practically dead."

Lucía glanced up at her, her brow furrowing. She set the notebook on her lap and quickly wrote.

"They're not dead. Just tired."

Beatriz blinked at the words, then rolled her eyes. "Tired? Roses don't get tired, Lucía. They're plants, not nuns."

Isabel chuckled from a few feet away. "Don't argue with her, Beatriz. Lucía's got a way of seeing things we don't."

Lucía ignored them, her focus narrowing to the roses. Her pen hovered over the page. She hesitated, her pulse quickening.

"Just this once," she thought. "It's harmless."

Lucía hesitated, her pulse quickening. Her pen hovered over the page, the word forming in her mind, sharp and deliberate. Finally, she wrote it:

"Bloom."

For a moment, nothing happened. The roses swayed gently in the breeze, their petals untouched by her command. Beatriz muttered something under her breath about the weather, already distracted. But Lucía stared at the bush, her heart pounding.

A single rose—just one—seemed to catch the light differently. Its edges softened, its color brightening ever so slightly, like the blush of dawn creeping over the horizon.

She blinked, unsure if she'd imagined it. Isabel glanced toward her but said nothing, her brow furrowed in curiosity.

Lucía quickly snapped the notebook shut, her breath hitching. She clutched it to her chest and turned away, the faint hum of power still lingering in her fingertips.

The silence that followed was heavy, though not laden with awe but with curiosity. Beatriz frowned, squinting at the bush. "Hmm. Did it always look like that?" she muttered, brushing her hand over the petals as if trying to confirm the subtle change.

Isabel tilted her head, her gaze flickering between Lucía and the roses. "What did you do?" she asked, her voice tinged with a mix of curiosity and suspicion.

Lucía's breath hitched. She clutched the notebook tighter, her heart racing. She quickly shook her head, her movements sharp but not panicked.

"Lucía," Isabel said softly, her tone patient but probing. "Something happened. I saw it. Was that... you?"

Lucía's face burned, but she refused to meet Isabel's gaze. Without another word, she spun on her heel and walked away, the notebook pressed against her chest like armor.

Isabel reached out, but Lucía flinched and turned, running toward the chapel.

The chapel was cool and dark, the faint scent of incense hanging in the air like an unanswered prayer. Shadows danced along the stone walls, shifting with the flicker of the eternal candle near the altar. Lucía sank to her knees before the altar, her breaths shallow and uneven, the soft scrape of her notebook against the floor the only sound in the stillness.

She opened the notebook with trembling hands, her fingers brushing the word she'd written earlier.

"Bloom."

The ink on the page seemed alive, shimmering faintly as though whispering back to her. It carried a weight she couldn't shake, a pull that both frightened and tempted her. Her heart pounded in her chest as she flipped to a blank page, her pen hesitating only for a moment before it moved, almost as if guided by something beyond her.

"Light," she wrote.

The candles on the altar flared to life instantly, their flames leaping high in a burst of brilliance before settling into a steady, golden glow. Lucía froze, staring at the gentle illumination she'd summoned, her hands gripping the edges of the notebook so tightly her knuckles turned white.

"Do you think you're the author of the world now, child?"

The voice, calm yet cutting, sliced through the silence. Lucía flinched and turned sharply to find Mother Superior standing at the entrance to the chapel. Her figure was shrouded in shadows, but her eyes, sharp and knowing, seemed to pierce through the dim light.

Lucía's heart sank. She grabbed her pen and scribbled furiously onto the page, holding the notebook up for Mother Superior to read.

"I didn't mean to."

Mother Superior stepped forward, her movements deliberate, her hands clasped before her. Her robes whispered against the stone floor as she knelt beside Lucía, her presence both grounding and overwhelming.

"What you mean to do is of little consequence, Lucía," she said, her tone carrying a gravity that weighed on the air itself. "The question is what you choose to do."

Lucía's eyes filled with tears, the words cutting through her turmoil like the toll of a bell. She wiped at her face hastily, the notebook trembling in her hands.

"Gifts," Mother Superior continued, her voice softening, "are neither sins nor blessings—not until you decide what they will become. That choice, child, is yours alone."

Lucía lowered her gaze, her pen hovering over the paper as her emotions churned. She wrote again, her strokes hesitant and uncertain.

"Why me?"

Mother Superior exhaled, the sound as gentle as the rustle of a page turning. "Why any of us?" she replied. "I have asked that question more times than I care to count. And I have learned this—God does not choose the easiest path for His strongest children. But He does not abandon them to walk it alone."

Lucía's tears spilled freely now, blurring the ink on the page. Her shoulders shook, her anguish spilling over in the only way it could. She wanted to scream, to tear the notebook apart, to cast it and its cursed power into the flames. But she couldn't.

Mother Superior reached out, her hand resting lightly on Lucía's shoulder. "Her silence is her strength," she said softly, her gaze steady. "But strength, untempered, is no more than raw power. And power without guidance is chaos. You cannot run from this, Lucía. If you do, it will consume you."

Lucía hesitated, her pen wavering above the paper. Then, slowly, she wrote two words.

"I'm scared."

"I know," Mother Superior whispered, her voice laced with an empathy that Lucía hadn't realized she needed. "Fear is not weakness, child. It is a call to faith. The world will try to make you believe your gift is a curse. It will test you. But you must remember this—

"Your words carry weight, child," Mother Superior said softly, her voice like a thread of calm in Lucía's storm. "Perhaps more than you know. God does not give such gifts lightly. Trust that in time, you will understand why."

The words wrapped around Lucía like a fragile comfort, fragile but real. She nodded slowly, her tears slowing as the weight of Mother Superior's presence anchored her.

"Come," Mother Superior said, rising gracefully. She extended a hand to Lucía. "Let us pray. For strength, for wisdom... and for the courage to wield what we are given."

Lucía took her hand, the warmth of it steadying her as she rose. For the first time, she felt a flicker of something besides fear—a faint glimmer of resolve. As the two knelt together before the altar, the light from the candles cast their shadows across the stone, intertwined yet distinct, as if to say that no path was walked entirely alone.

The day ended as it always did, cloaked in the solemn hush of prayer and the soft shuffle of the sisters retreating to their cells. But tonight, the stillness didn't comfort Lucía—it pressed down on her, heavy and stifling, as if the walls themselves were holding their breath. She lay awake in the darkness, her eyes wide and unblinking, the notebook resting beside her like a sentinel.

Her fingers traced its worn leather cover, a habit she didn't realize she'd formed. Tonight, it felt different, colder, heavier, almost alive. Questions swirled in her mind, restless and unspoken, each one louder than the last.

Unable to resist the pull, she opened the notebook, her fingers trembling as she flipped to a blank page. The pen hovered in her hand, suspended between fear and compulsion. Her heart raced as the word formed in her mind, unbidden but undeniable.

"Open."

She wrote it slowly, her strokes deliberate, each letter dragging her closer to something she couldn't name. The ink glistened on the page, almost too bright in the dim light, as if it carried its own glow. The air shifted, a sudden and subtle pressure that made her ears ring.

A sound—faint but distinct—cut through the silence. It was like a distant creak, the groan of old wood, or the whisper of hinges. Lucía froze, her breath catching in her throat as she glanced around the darkened room.

When nothing moved, she exhaled shakily, closing the notebook and clutching it to her chest. She shut her eyes tightly, willing sleep to come. But when it did, it brought no peace.

Her dreams were no longer of the garden or the sisters' hymns. Instead, she saw the gate, shrouded in mist, its edges pulsing with light. It loomed before her, vast and alive, its iron bars twisting into shapes she couldn't understand.

And then, it began to open.

2 |

The Call Beyond the Walls

The golden glow of evening bathed the convent in hues of warmth, yet Lucía felt only the weight of uncertainty pressing against her chest. She sat under the old oak tree, her notebook open on her lap. The garden buzzed faintly with life—birds chirping, the rustle of leaves in the breeze—but it felt distant, muted.

Her pen hovered above the page. Words filled her mind, clamoring to be written, yet none felt right. Finally, she scrawled the truth, simple and unadorned.

"I need to leave."

The ink glistened like a promise she couldn't break.

"Lucía?"

The voice startled her, and she quickly slammed the notebook shut. Sister Isabel stood nearby, her hands on her hips, her expression torn between curiosity and concern.

"You've been sitting here all day," Isabel said, stepping closer, her tone light but probing. "What's going on? And don't say 'nothing.' I can see it on your face—whatever it is, it's chewing you up inside."

Lucía clutched the notebook tightly to her chest, her eyes darting toward the horizon as if she could avoid Isabel's gaze.

"Don't even think about ignoring me," Isabel continued, planting herself in front of Lucía with an exaggerated sigh. "I'm not leaving until you talk to me—or, well, write to me. So, what is it? Did Sister Beatriz scold you again? Did you finally realize that her prized roses aren't worth all the fuss?"

Lucía hesitated, her grip tightening on the notebook. But Isabel's eyes were steady, kind but insistent.

"Lucía," Isabel said softly, her voice losing its teasing edge. "Please. What's bothering you?"

With a resigned sigh, Lucía opened the notebook. Her pen trembled as she wrote quickly, then turned the page toward Isabel.

"I need to leave."

Isabel blinked, the words hanging in the air like a challenge. "Leave?" she read aloud, her voice rising slightly. "Leave the convent?"

Lucía nodded, her expression unflinching.

"Why?" Isabel's tone softened, but her disbelief was clear. "Lucía, this is your home. You've never been outside these walls. What could possibly be waiting for you out there?"

Lucía's pen moved again, her strokes sharp and deliberate.

"I don't know. But I feel it. I have to go."

Isabel's face contorted with a mix of frustration and concern. She ran a hand through her hair, letting out a heavy sigh. "This is... this is crazy. Do you know what's out there? The world is harsh, Lucía. People don't care about kindness or faith—they'll eat you alive."

Lucía tilted her head, her expression calm but questioning, as if to say, *How do you know?*

"Oh, don't give me that look," Isabel said, throwing her hands up. "I've heard stories. And trust me, they don't end with happily ever after. There are no safety nets out there, Lucía. No quiet gardens, no chapel bells. Just noise, cruelty, and... and chaos."

Lucía stared at her, unshaken. Her pen moved again.

"I need to find out for myself."

"For what?" Isabel's voice cracked slightly, betraying the depth of her worry. "What's so important that you're willing to risk everything you've ever known?"

Lucía paused, her gaze dropping to the notebook. She hesitated, her pen hovering over the page as though searching for the right words. Finally, she wrote.

"I feel like I don't belong here anymore."

Isabel froze, the words hitting her like a blow. She opened her mouth to speak but closed it again, at a loss for what to say.

Lucía's pen moved again, her strokes more urgent now.

"I don't know what's out there. But I know I can't stay here. It feels... wrong."

Isabel crouched beside her, her voice low and strained. "Wrong? Lucía, this is where you've been loved, where you've been safe. Why would that feel wrong?"

Lucía hesitated, her fingers trembling as she wrote.

"It's not about love. It's about something else. Something bigger. I feel it, Isabel. Like I'm supposed to go. Like... like God is pulling me toward something, and I don't know what it is."

Isabel's breath hitched. She sat back on her heels, her gaze locked on Lucía's face. "God? You think this is from God?"

Lucía nodded, her eyes shining with conviction.

Isabel rubbed her temples, muttering under her breath. "Great. Fantastic. Divine intervention. As if this place didn't already have enough miracles to deal with."

Lucía's lips quirked into a faint, silent laugh.

"This isn't funny," Isabel shot back, though her tone softened as she looked at Lucía's face. "You're serious, aren't you? You really think you're meant to leave?"

Lucía nodded again, her gaze steady.

Isabel exhaled slowly, her shoulders sagging. "Fine. Let's see what Mother Superior has to say about this."

Lucía's brows furrowed, and she quickly scribbled a question.

"What if she says no?"

"She won't," Isabel said, though her voice wavered. "She's smarter than all of us combined. She'll know what to do."

As they rose to their feet, Isabel glanced at the notebook, her lips pressing into a thin line. "I don't like this, Lucía. Not one bit. But if you're going to do this, you're not doing it alone."

Lucía raised an eyebrow, her expression questioning.

"Oh, don't look at me like that," Isabel muttered. "Someone has to keep you from writing us into a catastrophe."

Lucía smiled faintly, the weight on her chest easing just a little. For the first time that day, she felt less alone.

Together, they walked toward the chapel, the glow of the setting sun casting long shadows behind them.

The chapel was dim, the eternal candle casting flickering shadows across the walls. The sisters were gathered in a semicircle, their faces lined with worry and determination. Whispers buzzed like restless bees, filling the sacred space with tension. Mother Superior sat at the front, her hands folded neatly, her face serene but unreadable, the weight of centuries of tradition resting on her shoulders.

Lucía stood to one side, her notebook clutched tightly against her chest like a shield. She glanced at the gathered sisters, their voices rising in a storm of conflicting beliefs.

Sister Beatriz was the first to speak, her voice sharp and cutting through the murmurs. "This is preposterous," she said, her hand slicing the air as if to dismiss the entire notion. "She's mute, for heaven's sake. How would she survive out there? She's never even set foot beyond the gates!"

"And that," Sister Ana countered, her tone measured but firm, "is exactly why we shouldn't stop her. If she feels called to leave, who are we to stand in her way? Free will is God's greatest gift."

Beatriz shot Ana a glare that could have wilted the strongest of roses. "Free will? Or foolishness? Let's not pretend she's ready for this. What if something happens to her? Who will take responsibility then? Not you, I imagine."

Ana didn't flinch, her eyes steady. "She's not a child, Beatriz. She has a right to make her own decisions."

"Rights mean nothing if she ends up lost or hurt!" Beatriz snapped back, her voice echoing through the stone walls.

"Are you saying God doesn't guide His children?" Ana retorted, her voice rising to match Beatriz's. "Do you think He would abandon Lucía now?"

"I think," Beatriz said, her tone biting, "that God gave us common sense for a reason. And my common sense tells me this is reckless."

"Enough!" Sister Patricia interjected, her voice trembling but resolute. "Why do we always assume the worst? What if this is God's will? What if she's meant to leave?"

Beatriz turned to Patricia, her expression a mix of frustration and disbelief. "And what if she's not? We're not talking about a stroll through the garden. This is the real world we're sending her into—cold, dangerous, and unforgiving. Do you really want that on your conscience?"

Patricia's hands twisted in her lap, her face pale. "But... but we can't cage her here. That's not our place."

The room erupted into a cacophony of voices, each sister arguing passionately for her stance. Some pleaded for caution, others championed Lucía's free will. The noise swelled, filling the sacred space with discord.

Lucía stood silently by the altar, her notebook held tightly against her chest. Her wide eyes darted between the women she had known her entire life, now locked in battle over her fate. Their love for her was unmistakable, but it was wrapped in layers of fear, faith, and conviction.

"Enough."

Mother Superior's voice cut through the clamor like a blade. The room fell silent instantly, the sisters turning toward her like chastised children. She rose slowly, her movements deliberate, her gaze sweeping over the gathered sisters.

"A decision has been made," she said, her tone calm but resolute, yet it carried the weight of finality. "Lucía may leave the convent if she chooses."

A gasp rippled through the room. Beatriz's lips parted to protest, but Mother Superior raised a hand, silencing her before she could utter a word.

"However," she continued, her eyes settling on Isabel, "she will not leave alone."

Isabel's breath caught, and she stiffened in her seat.

"As her caretaker and mentor, Sister Isabel," Mother Superior said, her gaze unwavering, "it will be your responsibility to accompany her. To guide her, protect her, and ensure that she is not lost in the world."

A stunned silence followed. The sisters exchanged wide-eyed glances, their earlier fervor replaced by shock. All eyes turned to Isabel, whose face had gone pale.

"Mother Superior," Beatriz began, her tone sharp, "surely you don't mean—"

"I do," Mother Superior interrupted, her voice firm but measured. "This is not a decision made lightly. But we have a responsibility to Lucía. If she is to leave, she must have someone by her side."

Isabel opened her mouth, but no words came out. She looked at Lucía, who clutched her notebook tightly, her expression both hopeful and apologetic.

Mother Superior stepped closer to Isabel, her tone softening. "You do not have to decide tonight. Pray. Reflect. Seek God's guidance. When you are ready, come to me. But understand this—should you choose to stay, it will be your divine duty to help Lucía find peace within these walls."

Isabel swallowed hard, her hands trembling as she nodded.

"Very well," Mother Superior said, her voice final. "This meeting is adjourned."

The sisters filed out slowly, their whispers filling the air like the rustling of leaves. Beatriz cast one last disapproving glance at Isabel before disappearing into the shadows. Ana placed a reassuring hand on Isabel's shoulder as she passed, murmuring, "Whatever you choose, we're here for you."

Isabel didn't respond. She sat frozen in her chair, the enormity of the situation settling over her like a weight she couldn't shake.

As the room emptied, Mother Superior lingered by the doorway, her gaze softening as she looked at Isabel. "Courage is not the absence of fear, Sister Isabel," she said gently. "It is the willingness to act despite it."

Isabel nodded mutely, her heart heavy as she glanced at Lucía, who offered her a small, hesitant smile.

When they were finally alone, Isabel whispered to herself, "What have I gotten myself into?"

A Leap of Faith

The moon hung high above the convent, bathing the stone walls in silver light that filtered through the narrow window of Sister Isabel's cell. Inside, the soft flicker of the eternal candle cast restless shadows on the walls, but they could not match the turmoil in her heart. Isabel sat on the edge of her cot, her veil folded neatly on the table beside her. The rosary dangled from her hands, the beads slipping rhythmically through her trembling fingers.

"God," she began, her voice barely a whisper, as though afraid the very air might shatter her fragile prayer. "I need You now. I need to hear You. I need to understand."

Her gaze lifted to the stars beyond the window, glittering like tiny messengers, too distant to offer the clarity she sought. Her words wavered, but she forced them out, rising from the depths of her uncertainty.

"You brought me here, Lord. You found me when I was lost, gave me this life, this purpose. You gave me sisters when I had no family, peace when I thought I'd never know it. And now... now You ask me to leave it all behind? To walk away from my vows, my home, my identity? Why, Lord? Why?"

Her voice cracked, tears pooling in her eyes as she searched the heavens for an answer that did not come. She clutched the rosary tighter, the cross digging into her palm, grounding her against the storm of emotions.

"How can I do this?" she asked, her voice breaking. "I am not strong enough. You see my heart, don't You? You know its weaknesses. What if I fail her? What if I fail You?"

Her chest rose and fell in uneven breaths as she bowed her head, her voice trembling. "I am afraid, Lord. Afraid to leave and afraid to stay. Afraid to step into a world I've never understood, a world that terrifies me. Afraid of what I'll become without this habit, without my vows. What am I without this life? What am I, Lord?"

She paused, the silence pressing against her, heavy and oppressive. Her tears fell freely now, each one a testament to the turmoil within her. She inhaled deeply, her fingers brushing the beads as she continued, her voice raw and unguarded.

"And Lucía..." Her voice softened as her mind turned to the young woman who had so unexpectedly reshaped her path. "She is so pure, so brave, so full of hope. She deserves someone who can guide her, someone wise and sure. Not me. Not this broken woman who questions everything. Why, Lord? Why have You chosen me for this? How can I be enough for her?"

The weight of her inadequacy pressed down on her shoulders, bending her until she rested her forehead against her clasped hands. Her words spilled out, desperate, pleading. "I don't know how to do this. I don't know how to leave, and I don't know how to stay. I don't know how to be the person she needs, the person You ask me to be."

Her sobs filled the small room, raw and unrestrained, until she forced herself to still, breathing deeply, clutching the rosary as though it were a lifeline. She closed her eyes tightly, her voice dropping to a whisper. "But if this is Your will, Lord... if this is truly what

You ask of me, then give me the courage to follow. I don't ask for answers. I don't ask for clarity. Just the strength to take the next step."

The silence in the room deepened, and for a moment, it felt as though the entire world was holding its breath. The flickering light of the eternal candle seemed to soften, its glow wrapping gently around Isabel like a fragile embrace. A faint sense of peace—tentative, but real—began to settle in her heart, like the first rays of dawn breaking through the night.

Her tears slowed, though her hands still trembled. Slowly, Isabel rose from her knees, her joints aching, her spirit heavy but steadier. She turned toward the small mirror above the washbasin, catching sight of her reflection. The woman staring back at her was weary, her face marked by the weight of her decision.

Isabel rose slowly, her knees stiff and her body aching, but her spirit steadier. She turned to the small table where her veil lay, the fabric still as familiar as her own skin. She reached for it instinctively but stopped mid-motion. Her hand hovered, her decision crystallizing.

No.

With deliberate movements, she folded the veil more tightly and placed it atop the rest of her habits. Her gaze caught her reflection in the tiny, tarnished mirror above the washbasin. She stared at herself—the sister she had been—and then, as if drawn by an unseen hand, she reached for the small pair of scissors she kept for trimming thread.

Her hands were steady now as the blades met her hair. Snip. Snip. Dark locks fell to the floor, one after another, until her reflection no longer looked like Sister Isabel. The woman staring back at her was someone new, someone unbound by vows, someone she barely recognized yet knew deeply.

Her fingertips brushed over her face, hesitant but sure, tracing the curves of her cheeks, her lips. She opened a small wooden chest she had almost forgotten she owned and removed a simple dress, tucked away as a keepsake of her youth. The fabric felt strange against her skin, softer, freer.

A modest tube of lipstick, years old but still vibrant, emerged from the chest. She hesitated for only a moment before swiping a delicate touch of color across her lips. It felt daring, transformative.

When she stepped back from the mirror, she caught her breath. Not from vanity, but from the startling realization of who she saw. For the first time in decades, she wasn't Sister Isabel. She was simply Isabel.

"Isabel," she whispered aloud, testing the name without the weight of her title. It felt strange. It felt right.

She took a deep, steadying breath and left her cell, her footsteps soft but purposeful as she made her way through the quiet halls. The air seemed different tonight—charged, expectant. The eternal candle's light flickered as she passed, as though it, too, recognized her transformation.

When she reached Mother Superior's office, she hesitated for only a moment before knocking gently. A calm voice called from within. "Enter."

Isabel stepped inside, her breath hitching as Mother Superior looked up from her desk. For a moment, neither woman spoke. Mother Superior's eyes scanned Isabel, taking in the simple dress, the cropped hair, the faint blush of lipstick. Slowly, she rose to her feet.

"I see you have made a decision," Mother Superior said, her voice steady but laced with something softer pride, perhaps, or sorrow.

Silence enveloped the room like a sacred shroud, the air thick with the unspoken weight of the moment. Isabel stood just inside the doorway, her breaths uneven, her hands trembling at her sides.

Across the desk, Mother Superior regarded her with a stillness that spoke of both sorrow and strength.

Finally, the older woman moved, her hands deliberate as she reached for a worn leather folder resting on the desk. The sound of it opening seemed to echo in the stillness, the faint rustle of papers carrying the weight of years. Inside were the records of Sister Isabel's life of devotion, sacrifice, and purpose.

Mother Superior's voice broke the silence, low and steady, each word landing like a gentle yet irrevocable bell toll. "By the power vested in me," she began, her gaze unwavering, "I close your life as a nun in this convent. I place you now, Isabel, fully and completely in God's hands. He will guide you as He always has, but now, on a path that lies beyond these walls."

The finality of her words hung between them, but there was no harshness, only a deep and abiding compassion. She paused, her eyes softening as they rested on Isabel, who stood frozen in place, her breath catching in her throat.

"Remember," Mother Superior continued, her tone gentler now, "this is not the last decision you will face. There are others waiting ahead—decisions that God Himself will place before you. Decisions that only you, Isabel, can make."

Isabel's throat tightened as she tried to respond, but her words faltered. She opened her mouth to speak, but nothing came, only the shimmer of tears pooling in her eyes.

Mother Superior's gaze shifted, lingering on Isabel's face. Her lips parted, and her voice softened, almost a whisper, as if the words were meant only for her. "My God," she murmured, her tone a mixture of wonder and grief, "you are a beautiful woman, Isabel."

The simplicity of the words shattered Isabel's composure. A sob escaped her lips, raw and unguarded, as she crossed the room in a few desperate steps. She fell into Mother Superior's arms, clutching at her as though she were an anchor in the storm of her emotions. Her tears flowed freely, soaking into the older woman's shoulder, and Mother Superior held her tightly, her hands stroking Isabel's back in a gesture both maternal and divine.

Neither spoke; the silence between them carried more weight than words ever could. It was a silence filled with love, with pain, and with a sacred understanding that transcended language.

After a time, Isabel pulled back, her face streaked with tears, her breath trembling. Mother Superior raised her hands and cupped Isabel's face, her palms warm and steady against her cheeks.

"Trust God, Isabel," she said, her voice a benediction, quiet yet unyielding. "He will always bring you closer to Him, even when the path is unclear. Even when it feels impossible."

Isabel closed her eyes, leaning into the touch as a fresh wave of tears slipped down her face. She nodded, her lips quivering as she whispered, "I will."

Mother Superior's hands lingered for a moment longer before she stepped back, releasing Isabel with a soft, almost reluctant sigh. Isabel straightened, wiping her tears as she turned toward the door. Her steps, though hesitant, were steady, her shoulders squared with the quiet resolve of someone stepping into the unknown.

Mother Superior watched her leave, her heart aching with both pride and loss. As the door closed softly behind Isabel, she whispered into the quiet room, her words carried upward like a prayer. "Go with God, my child. May He keep you always in His light."

4 |

Into the World Beyond

The gates of the convent stood tall and silent, their iron bars entwined with ivy, shimmering faintly in the first light of dawn. They had always been more than gates—they were a boundary, a sanctuary, a threshold that few ever crossed. This morning, they would open for Isabel and Lucía, casting them into a world neither had touched in years, if ever.

The courtyard was eerily quiet, save for the distant cooing of doves perched on the chapel roof. The sisters were absent from the steps, their places empty by design. But from the narrow windows of their cells, faint outlines and discreet movements betrayed their presence. Behind the curtains, many clutched rosaries, whispered prayers, or simply stood in silent vigil, their faces streaked with emotion.

At the gate stood Mother Superior, alone but unyielding, her figure outlined against the pale gray of the morning sky. Her hands rested lightly on the iron latch, as though she could hold back the inevitable just a moment longer.

Isabel and Lucía approached, their footsteps hesitant but resolute. Isabel's hair was short now, a modest crop framing her face. Her simple dress moved with her steps, unfamiliar yet liberating. Lucía, clutching her notebook as though it were armor, walked slightly behind her, her eyes darting toward the surrounding windows, sensing the love and unease that flowed unseen from within the convent walls.

Mother Superior's gaze swept over them, lingering on each as though memorizing their faces. She broke the silence, her voice even yet tinged with tenderness.

"You are ready," she said, though it wasn't a question.

Isabel took a breath, steadying herself. "As ready as I'll ever be."

Mother Superior's lips curved into a faint, knowing smile. "None of us is ever truly ready, Isabel. The important thing is that you are willing. And that is enough."

Lucía's grip on her notebook tightened. Mother Superior turned to her, her expression softening further. "Lucía," she said gently, "your journey is just beginning. It will not always be easy. There will be days when you doubt yourself, days when you question why God has chosen this path for you. But in those moments, remember this—you are not walking alone. He is with you, always. And so is she." She gestured subtly toward Isabel, her meaning clear.

Lucía blinked rapidly, her emotions betraying her usual composure. She quickly scribbled in her notebook and held it up for both to see.

"What if I fail?"

Mother Superior's gaze didn't waver. "Failure is not falling, child. Failure is refusing to rise again. And you," she said, her voice carrying the weight of unshakable belief, "are stronger than you know. Strong enough to rise, again and again."

Isabel glanced at Lucía, her heart aching at the vulnerability in her young companion's face. She placed a steadying hand on her shoulder. "We'll figure it out," she said softly. "Together."

Mother Superior nodded approvingly; her hands clasped in front of her. She turned her full attention to Isabel now, the moment shifting. "And you, Isabel," she began, her tone almost imperceptibly deeper, "you have always been a beacon in this convent—a sister, a guide, a source of strength. You are leaving behind these walls, but you are not leaving your purpose. That purpose will follow you, change you, challenge you in ways you cannot yet see."

Isabel exhaled slowly. "I hope I'm enough," she said, her voice barely above a whisper.

Mother Superior stepped closer, resting a hand lightly on Isabel's shoulder. "You will find," she said, her eyes searching Isabel's, "that God's measure of enough is different from our own. You don't need to know every answer. You don't need to carry the weight of every decision alone. But you must trust—trust that the path you walk will reveal itself, one step at a time."

Isabel nodded, her throat tight with emotion. She opened her mouth to speak, but before she could, Mother Superior continued, her tone shifting slightly, almost imperceptibly.

"There will be other decisions, Isabel," she said. "Decisions that will test your faith, your strength, your very understanding of who you are. When those moments come, remember this—God does not give us more than we can bear. But He does ask us to trust Him, especially when the burden feels impossible."

A faint flicker of uneasy crossed Isabel's face, but she nodded again, her resolve firming.

Mother Superior stepped back slightly, her voice rising just enough to carry over the distant hum of the waking world. "Both of you," she said, addressing them together now, "carry something sacred within you. Protect it. Nurture it. And trust that it will guide you, even when the way is unclear"

She raised her hands in a gesture of blessing, her voice taking on the cadence of a prayer. "May the Lord bless you and keep you. May He guide your steps and protect your hearts. May He grant you courage in the face of fear and wisdom in the face of doubt. Go in peace, my children, for you do not go alone."

The blessing lingered in the air as she stepped forward and grasped the gate's iron latch. The sound of the hinges creaking open was both a beginning and an end.

Beyond the gates, a taxi waited, its engine idling softly, its headlights cutting through the morning mist.

Mother Superior looked at them one final time, her gaze filled with a mixture of pride, sorrow, and an unshakable faith. "Go now," she said quietly. "And remember—you are loved, no matter where this path takes you."

Isabel and Lucía stepped through the gates together, their shoulders brushing as they crossed the threshold.

Lucía turned briefly, her eyes meeting Mother Superior's, the notebook clutched tightly in her hands. She didn't write anything; she didn't need to. Her gaze spoke all the words she couldn't.

Isabel hesitated, her hand resting on the open taxi door. "Thank you," she said softly, her voice steady despite the tremble in her hands. "For everything."

Mother Superior inclined her head, her expression serene. "You are ready," she said simply.

The two climbed into the taxi, the door closing with a soft click. The engine rumbled, the car rolling forward slowly, its tires crunching over gravel.

Mother Superior stood at the gates, her hands clasped, watching until the taxi disappeared into the mist. Only then did she turn, closing the gates with a deliberate motion.

She rested her forehead briefly against the cool iron, whispering a prayer so quiet even the wind couldn't carry it. "Guide them, Lord," she murmured. "Keep them safe. And bring them closer to You."

Above, the sisters in their windows remained motionless, their prayers rising like incense. Below, the courtyard was empty again, save for the lone figure of Mother Superior walking slowly back toward the chapel.

In the taxi, Lucía gazed out at the unfolding world, her eyes wide with wonder and trepidation. Beside her, Isabel sat stiffly, her hands gripping her lap, her thoughts a storm of fear and faith.

Finally, Isabel glanced at Lucía, her voice soft but firm. "This is it," she said. "The first step."

Lucía met her gaze, her fingers brushing the edge of her notebook. She nodded.

And together, they moved forward, into the unknown.

The taxi ride was quiet save for the occasional bump in the road. Isabel and Lucía sat side by side, the weight of their journey pressing down on them in different ways. Lucía clutched her notebook tightly, her fingers brushing its worn edges as though drawing strength from it. Isabel sat straighter than usual, her hands clasped tightly in her lap, her eyes darting to the window as the world passed by in a blur of unfamiliarity.

When the taxi pulled up in front of the shelter, the starkness of the building made them pause. The structure was modest—a two-story brick building with large, welcoming windows. The words *"St. Raphael's Shelter for Women"* were etched on a weathered sign hanging above the door. The soft light spilling from the windows cast a warm glow against the early morning fog.

Isabel stepped out first, smoothing her dress and glancing back at Lucía, who hesitated before following. She could feel Lucía's unease, the tension in her posture as she clutched the notebook even tighter.

"Come on," Isabel said gently, offering a small smile. "We're in this together, remember?"

Lucía nodded hesitantly, her wide eyes scanning their surroundings.

Inside, the shelter bustled with quiet activity. Women moved through the modestly furnished common area, their voices low and their movements purposeful. The smell of freshly brewed coffee and warm bread filled the air, mingling with the faint scent of lavender that clung to the well-worn furniture.

A woman in her late forties approached them, her face kind but lined with the wear of responsibility. Her hair was pulled back into a loose bun, and she wore a simple cardigan over a floral dress. Her sharp yet warm eyes took in Isabel and Lucía with a quick, assessing glance.

"Hello," she said, her voice even but welcoming. "I'm Maria. I run this shelter. You must be the women Mother Superior told me about."

Isabel nodded, stepping forward and extending her hand. "Yes, I'm Isabel, and this is Lucía. We've come from the convent."

Maria shook Isabel's hand firmly, then glanced at Lucía, who offered a polite but silent nod.

"Mother Superior spoke highly of you both," Maria said, her tone light but sincere. "She told me to expect you this morning. Let me show you around and get you settled. We're happy to have you here, though I'll need to be honest—we don't have a lot of space, and our time together may be short. We take in many women, and we're always in need of room for those who come through our doors."

"We understand," Isabel said quickly. "We won't be here long. Just until we can... figure out our next steps."

Maria nodded, her expression softening. "That's what this place is for. A start. Come with me."

She led them through the modest common room, pointing out the basics. "Here's the kitchen," she said, gesturing to a bright space where a few women were chatting over steaming mugs of tea. "You're welcome to use it during meal times. We keep the pantry stocked as best we can, but everyone pitches in to make sure we have enough to go around."

Lucía's eyes wandered, taking in the unfamiliar sight of so many women, some laughing softly, others carrying the weight of unspoken stories.

"And this is the sleeping area," Maria continued, leading them down a narrow hallway. She stopped at a small room with two neatly made cots and a single wooden chair. "It's not much, but it's yours for now. Clean towels are on the chair, and there's space for your things under the beds."

"It's perfect," Isabel said, her voice warm with gratitude. "Thank you, Maria. Truly."

Maria offered a faint smile. "You're welcome. Make yourselves comfortable, and when you're ready, come back to the common room. I'd like to talk a bit more about what you'll need and how we can help."

As Maria turned to leave, Lucía hesitated, then scribbled something in her notebook. She tapped Maria lightly on the arm, then held up the page.

"Thank you for helping us."

Maria read the words and smiled warmly. "You're welcome, Lucía. And don't worry. You're in good hands here."

Lucía nodded, her cheeks flushing slightly as Maria walked away.

Once alone in the room, Isabel sat heavily on one of the cots, exhaling a breath she hadn't realized she'd been holding. "Well," she said, glancing at Lucía, "here we are. Step one."

Lucía placed her notebook carefully on the chair and sat down on the edge of the opposite cot. Her gaze lingered on the small window, where sunlight filtered through a thin curtain.

"Are you okay?" Isabel asked softly.

Lucía picked up her notebook, hesitated, then began to write. She held it up for Isabel to read.

"It feels strange. I don't know what to do."

Isabel nodded, her expression thoughtful. "That makes two of us," she admitted, a faint smile tugging at her lips. "But we'll figure it out. One step at a time."

Lucía's gaze flickered toward Isabel, her eyes filled with questions she couldn't quite put into words. She wrote again.

"Do you think we made the right choice?"

Isabel paused, her eyes searching Lucía's face. "I don't know," she said honestly. "But I think the fact that we're here means we're supposed to be. And whatever happens next... we'll face it together."

Lucía nodded slowly, though the uncertainty in her expression remained.

"Come on," Isabel said, standing and brushing off her dress. "Let's head back to the common room. Maybe Maria can give us some advice on where to start."

Lucía hesitated, her gaze flickering to her notebook before she slowly rose, clutching it tightly to her chest as if it were a shield. As they walked toward the door, Isabel cast a curious glance at her, her lips quirking into a faint smile.

"You know, I've always been curious, Lucía," Isabel began, her tone casual but tinged with genuine interest. "You write so much in that notebook, but I've never seen you change it because you've filled it up completely. How is that possible?"

Lucía paused mid-step, turning to Isabel with a thoughtful expression. She flipped the notebook open, her pen moving deliberately across the page. A moment later, she held it up for Isabel to read.

"The words or phrases disappear after a few minutes. But nobody else can write in this book."

Isabel blinked, taken aback. She leaned in slightly, reading the words again as if she might have misunderstood them. "They... disappear?" she asked, her voice laced with wonder. "And no one else can write in it? Not even me?"

Lucía shook her head firmly, a faint smile playing on her lips.

Isabel stared at the notebook, her mind racing with questions she couldn't quite articulate. Finally, she exhaled, shaking her head in disbelief. "Well," she said with a soft laugh, "I guess that's just another mystery to add to the list."

Lucía's smile widened slightly, and she gave Isabel a knowing look as they continued toward the common room. Whatever secrets the notebook held, it seemed they would have to reveal themselves in their own time.

5

The First Steps

The hum of life outside the convent walls had been a quiet, distant murmur before. Now it was a roar. Cars whizzed by, voices echoed off the brick walls of narrow city streets, and the smells—oh, the smells! Fried food, fresh bread, exhaust fumes, and something Isabel couldn't quite place but fervently hoped was not garbage.

Isabel and Lucía stood at the corner of a bustling street, the sunlight glinting off the glass storefronts. Lucía clutched her notebook to her chest like a talisman, her wide eyes darting from one spectacle to the next. Isabel, on the other hand, was trying—and failing—not to look like a deer caught in headlights.

"Okay," Isabel said, exhaling slowly. "Maria suggested we start with groceries. That seems... manageable. A little food, some basic supplies. Easy enough, right?"

Lucía tilted her head, her gaze shifting to the large sign across the street that read "Supermart." She raised an eyebrow as if to say, *Are you sure about that?*

"Don't give me that look," Isabel muttered, squaring her shoulders. "How hard can it be?"

They stepped into the store, greeted immediately by the sound of clinking carts and the faint hum of a pop song playing overhead.

Isabel froze, staring at the sheer enormity of the place. Shelves stretched endlessly, stacked with items she couldn't even name.

"This is... bigger than the convent's entire garden," she whispered.

Lucía tugged at Isabel's sleeve and pointed to a nearby aisle labeled "Fresh Produce." They maneuvered their way over, bumping into an elderly woman's cart on the way.

"Sorry!" Isabel blurted, her cheeks flushing.

The woman smiled kindly. "First time shopping?"

Isabel nodded sheepishly. "That obvious?"

"Don't worry, dear. We've all been there," the woman said before moving on, leaving Isabel to whisper under her breath, "Not *this* far, I bet."

As they reached the produce section, Isabel picked up a tomato and frowned. "So, we just... grab what we need? No prayers, no blessings?"

Lucía nodded and gestured toward the plastic bags. Isabel struggled to pull one open, shaking it vigorously until it finally obeyed.

"Victory!" Isabel exclaimed, earning a soft laugh from Lucía.

"Okay, now what?" Isabel said, glancing at the array of fruits and vegetables. Lucía wrote quickly in her notebook and held it up: *What do you want to eat?*

"Good question," Isabel muttered, staring helplessly at a pile of zucchinis. "Do they sell recipes with these things?"

Lucía rolled her eyes, her lips curving into a silent laugh. She picked out a few apples and handed them to Isabel.

"Oh, good. Something I recognize," Isabel said, dropping them into the bag.

They moved through the store, Lucía occasionally scribbling notes to Isabel about what they needed while Isabel struggled to decipher brand names and figure out how much anything cost.

"Why does bread have to be *artisan*?" Isabel grumbled at one point. "What's wrong with just... bread?"

Lucía shrugged, biting back another laugh.

Finally, they reached the checkout line, where Isabel stared in horror as the cashier rang up their items.

"Thirty-two dollars?" she whispered to Lucía. "For food? Do they think we're feeding an army?"

Lucía wrote quickly in her notebook: *It's normal.*

"Normal?" Isabel scoffed, fumbling with the cash Maria had given her. "I feel like we're being robbed."

The cashier gave them an amused glance as they hurriedly packed their items and left the store.

At St. Raphael's Shelter

Back at the shelter, Isabel and Lucía entered the modest kitchen with their grocery bags. The room hummed with quiet activity. A few women moved between counters, preparing meals or chatting softly in groups. The scent of freshly brewed coffee mingled with the aroma of a warm stew bubbling on the stove. The murmur of conversation paused momentarily as curious eyes turned toward the new arrivals.

"First time grocery shopping?" a young woman with curly red hair asked, her grin teasing but kind. She was slicing carrots at a nearby counter, her hands quick and practiced.

"First time in *forever*," Isabel admitted, shaking her head with a rueful smile as she placed the bags on the counter. "Do they charge by the slice of bread these days, or is it just my imagination?"

The woman laughed. "Wait until you try to buy eggs. You might need a loan."

Lucía's lips twitched into a silent chuckle as she set down her own bag, meticulously lining up its contents.

Maria entered the room just then, her sharp gaze immediately zeroing in on Isabel's overwhelmed expression. "How was your first outing?" she asked, her lips twitching with amusement.

"Oh, it was... educational," Isabel replied, dumping a bag of apples onto the counter with exaggerated flair. "Did you know bread now costs as much as wine used to?"

Maria chuckled, crossing her arms. "Welcome to the world, Sister Isabel."

Isabel hesitated, her hand brushing over the fabric of her dress. "Not a sister anymore," she said softly, her voice laced with a bittersweet mix of acceptance and loss.

Maria's expression softened. She placed a reassuring hand on Isabel's arm. "You'll adjust," she said gently. "It takes time, but you will. We all do."

Lucía, ever watchful, tapped Maria on the shoulder and held up her notebook:

Where should we look for a place to live?

Maria leaned against the counter, considering the question. "That depends," she said thoughtfully. "What's your budget? What kind of place are you looking for?"

"Affordable," Isabel said dryly. "And, uh, not falling apart."

"Well, that narrows it down," Maria replied with a smirk. "I know a few landlords who might have openings. A couple of them can be... let's just say, colorful characters. You up for it?"

Isabel glanced at Lucía, who nodded firmly, her eyes betraying both apprehension and determination. "We're up for it," Isabel said with equal resolve.

Adapting to Shelter Life

Over the next few days, Isabel and Lucía found themselves slowly adjusting to the rhythms of life at St. Raphael's. The shelter was a blend of bustling activity and quiet moments of shared reflection.

The common room served as the heart of the building, with its mismatched furniture and walls adorned with cheerful, if faded, murals.

Isabel found herself sitting at one of the communal tables one afternoon, folding laundry alongside Maria and a woman named Ruth, whose short-cropped hair and no-nonsense demeanor contrasted with her gentle voice.

"So, what brought you here?" Ruth asked, her tone casual but not prying.

Isabel hesitated, glancing at Lucía, who was seated across the room, absorbed in her notebook. "It's... a long story," she said finally, her hands pausing over a neatly folded shirt. "Let's just say we're starting over."

Ruth nodded knowingly. "A lot of us are."

"Isabel used to be a nun," Maria added, her tone light but affectionate.

Ruth's eyebrows shot up. "Really? And you're out here folding socks with the rest of us sinners?"

Isabel laughed, surprised by the comment. "Guess so. God works in mysterious ways, doesn't He?"

Ruth grinned, her warm laughter mingling with Isabel's. "That He does."

A Moment of Connection

Later that evening, the shelter's residents gathered in the common room for their nightly tea. Isabel sat with her cup, watching Lucía from across the room. The young woman was perched on the windowsill, her notebook balanced on her knees. Her pen moved quickly, almost feverishly, as though she were trying to capture something fleeting.

Maria settled into the chair beside Isabel, cradling her own mug. "She writes a lot," she said softly.

"She always has," Isabel replied. "That notebook is her lifeline."

Maria studied Lucía for a moment. "She doesn't talk?"

"No," Isabel said, shaking her head. "But she says everything she needs to with that notebook."

Lucía glanced up, sensing their conversation, and offered a small smile before returning to her writing.

Maria leaned closer to Isabel, her voice dropping to a whisper. "You're protective of her."

Isabel nodded, her gaze fixed on Lucía. "She's... special. I don't know how to explain it. It's like she carries something inside her that the world needs. But the world can be so..." She trailed off, searching for the right word.

"Cruel," Maria finished for her.

Isabel exhaled heavily. "Yes. And I want to make sure she's ready for it."

Maria reached out and squeezed Isabel's hand. "You're doing fine. You both are."

Nighttime Conversations

The room was quiet, wrapped in the soft hum of the city beyond the shelter walls. A streetlamp outside the window cast faint, shifting shadows across the small space, mingling with the muted sounds of distant cars and occasional footsteps from the hallway.

Isabel lay stretched on her cot, her hands resting behind her head as she stared at the ceiling. Lucía sat cross-legged on her bed, her notebook balanced on her knees, the familiar scratching of her pen the only sound breaking the silence between them.

"Lucía," Isabel said, her voice cutting through the stillness, soft but purposeful.

Lucía glanced up, her brows arching in silent acknowledgment.

"I've been thinking," Isabel began, turning on her side to face Lucía. "This whole journey we're on—it's terrifying, exciting, and completely insane. Don't you think?"

Lucía tilted her head, a faint smirk tugging at the corners of her mouth. She began to write, her strokes deliberate but quick, and then turned the notebook toward Isabel: *Isn't that what faith is?*

Isabel let out a low laugh, shaking her head. "You and your one-liners. Always so sure of yourself, huh?"

Lucía shrugged, her smile widening. She scribbled again and held it up: *No. I just act like I am.*

Isabel chuckled, a rare, light sound that filled the room. "Well, you're fooling me," she said, sitting up and swinging her legs over the edge of the cot. "You know, you're lucky you're good with that notebook. Sometimes, I wish I had something like it to figure out my thoughts."

Lucía's pen hovered, her expression thoughtful before she wrote again: *What would you write if you had one?*

Isabel paused, taken aback by the question. She glanced at the window, the faint light playing across her face. "I don't know," she said slowly. "Maybe all the things I'm scared to say out loud. All the doubts I keep tucked away."

Lucía's pen scratched softly across the page, and she held up her reply: *What scares you?*

The question hung between them, heavier than it should've been. Isabel exhaled, her shoulders sagging slightly. "Honestly? That I'm going to mess this up. That I'll let you down. That we'll end up with nothing to show for all this."

Lucía frowned, her gaze steady and probing. She turned back to her notebook and wrote: *You won't let me down.*

Isabel's laugh was sharp, almost bitter. "How can you be so sure? You're the one dragging me forward half the time."

Lucía shook her head and wrote again: *You've been strong for me in ways I can't be. That's enough.*

Isabel's chest tightened as she read the words. "You really believe that, don't you?" she asked, her voice softer now.

Lucía nodded firmly, then added: *I don't need you to be perfect. Just present.*

The simplicity of the statement left Isabel momentarily speechless. She ran a hand through her cropped hair, her thoughts swirling. Finally, she managed a quiet, "Thanks."

Lucía reached out, placing her notebook beside her and patting the space on the cot. Isabel hesitated for only a second before moving to sit beside her.

"You know," Isabel began, glancing sideways at Lucía, "I was thinking about how much you write in that notebook. Have you ever wondered what your life would be like if you couldn't write? If this wasn't your way of speaking?"

Lucía looked at her with wide, questioning eyes, then picked up the notebook and wrote: *I don't think about it. This is part of who I am.*

Isabel nodded slowly. "Fair enough. But you've never wondered what it'd be like to just... speak? To not need the notebook?"

Lucía's pen hesitated, then moved carefully across the page: *Sometimes. But I think words are more than just sounds. They're power. They're choice. This way... they're mine.*

The depth of the statement caught Isabel off guard. She studied Lucía's face, her quiet determination, and the serene conviction that seemed to radiate from her. "You're stronger than I'll ever be," Isabel murmured.

Lucía shook her head, smiling faintly. She wrote: *We're strong in different ways.*

Isabel snorted softly. "Still a smart aleck, even in writing."

Lucía's laugh was silent but contagious, lighting up her face in a way that made Isabel grin despite herself.

"Come on," Isabel said after a moment, stretching as she stood. "Let's get some rest. We've got another big day tomorrow."

Lucía nodded, tucking the notebook beneath her pillow with care. As Isabel settled back onto her cot, she watched Lucía close her eyes, her face peaceful yet pensive.

Before the room fell into full silence, Isabel whispered, "Thanks for keeping me grounded, Lucía."

Lucía's lips curved in a soft, knowing smile, even as sleep began to claim her.

Apartment Hunting

Their first stop was a small apartment building on the edge of town. The building's exterior was as weary as the wiry man who greeted them—a landlord with a thick mustache, a cigarette balanced precariously on his lip, and a demeanor that screamed impatience.

"You're here about the place?" he barked, not waiting for a reply. "Come on, I don't got all day."

The building smelled faintly of dampness and neglect, the kind of place where corners were cut and tenants were forgotten. The apartment was tiny, with peeling wallpaper and a ceiling fan that hung precariously from its mount. Lucía wrinkled her nose, clutching her notebook tightly, while Isabel tried to muster politeness.

"What's the rent?" Isabel asked, her tone cautious.

"Eight hundred a month, plus utilities," the landlord said gruffly, scratching his chin.

"Eight hundred?" Isabel repeated, incredulous. She gestured vaguely at the stained carpet and cracked tiles. "For this?"

"Take it or leave it," he replied with a shrug, his tone making it clear he couldn't care less.

"We'll... think about it," Isabel said, grabbing Lucía's arm before she could scribble something in her notebook that might provoke the man.

Once outside, Isabel let out a heavy sigh. "First lesson of apartment hunting," she muttered. "Everything looks worse in person."

Lucía scribbled a quick note and showed it to her: And it smelled bad.

Isabel snorted, her mood lightening. "Yes, it did."

Their second stop was even worse. A basement unit in a blocky, soulless building, it felt more like a dungeon than a home. The single room was windowless, dimly lit, and inexplicably damp.

The landlord, a disheveled man wearing socks with sandals, waved at the space with little ceremony. "It's cozy," he said.

Lucía shot Isabel a skeptical glance, then began writing in her notebook.

Isabel glanced at the words and quickly cleared her throat, intercepting the message before the landlord could see. "We'll, uh, let you know," she said hastily, hustling Lucía out before she could escalate the situation.

The third stop offered a glimmer of hope.

The door opened to reveal a cheerful woman in her sixties with an infectious smile and a brightly colored scarf that looked like it belonged to a watercolor painting. "Welcome!" she said, her voice warm and welcoming. "Come in, come in. It's not much, but it's cozy."

The apartment was small but immaculate, with sunlight streaming through lace curtains that framed a view of a small park across the street. A faint scent of lavender lingered in the air, and the furniture, though sparse, was well-kept and inviting.

Lucía wandered to the window, her expression softening as she gazed out at the park. Children played under the trees, their laughter rising faintly through the glass.

"What's the rent?" Isabel asked, cautiously optimistic.

"Six fifty," the woman said. "And I don't charge extra for pets if you ever get one. I've got two cats myself—Biscuit and Gravy."

Lucía smiled, her eyes brightening as she quickly wrote in her notebook: This feels right.

Isabel read the note, her heart lifting for the first time that day. "We'll take it," she said, glancing at Lucía, who nodded in agreement.

The woman beamed. "Wonderful! I'll get the paperwork ready. Welcome to your new home."

But the optimism was short-lived.

Their next stop was a sprawling, aging apartment complex on the rougher side of town. The landlord, a broad-shouldered man with a leering grin, met them at the door. His shirt was unbuttoned just a little too far, and his cologne was suffocating.

"Ladies," he said, his tone oily. "You're gonna love this place. Come on, let me show you the view first—it's spectacular." He gestured toward the stairwell. "Take her up to the rooftop," he said to Lucía, flashing a toothy grin. "You've never seen the city like this."

Lucía hesitated, glancing at Isabel, who nodded reassuringly. "Go on," Isabel said. "I'll check out the apartment."

As Lucía made her way up the stairs, the landlord led Isabel into the dimly lit unit. The moment they were alone, his demeanor shifted. His grin widened as he moved closer. "So, what do you think?" he asked, his voice low and suggestive.

Isabel stiffened, the warning bells in her mind blaring. "It's... not bad," she said cautiously, stepping back.

But he closed the distance, his hand brushing her arm. Before she could react, he leaned in, his lips pressing against hers. Isabel froze, her mind racing. Fighting back could draw Lucía's attention, and she didn't want to risk her knowing.

"Stop," she managed, her voice trembling.

The sound of footsteps saved her. Lucía burst into the room, her eyes wide and sharp as she took in the scene. The landlord immediately stepped back, his grin faltering under Lucía's piercing gaze.

For the first time in her life, Lucía felt anger erupt within her, hot and unrelenting. She reached for her notebook, her hand steady despite the storm raging in her chest. She wrote in bold, forceful strokes: PAY AND REPENT.

The landlord's smirk disappeared as he fell to his knees, clutching his chest.. A strangled scream tore from his throat as his body convulsed, his face contorted in a grotesque mask of pain.

"Lucía, stop it!" Isabel shouted, her voice cutting through the chaos.

Lucía's pen moved again, her jaw tight: HE NEEDS TO PAY AND REPENT.

"No, Lucía," Isabel said, stepping forward. Her voice trembled but held firm. "You are not God. Stop this. Right now."

Lucía hesitated, her pen hovering over the page. Her eyes burned with tears of fury and confusion.

"Please," Isabel said, softer now. "This isn't who you are."

With a shaky breath, Lucía wrote a single word: STOP.

The man collapsed onto the floor, gasping for air. He scrambled to the corner of the room, his face pale with terror. "Who... who are you?" he stammered, his voice hoarse. "Witches... get out of my place. For God's sake, GET OUT!"

Isabel grabbed Lucía's hand, pulling her toward the door. "Come on," she said sharply, her voice cracking.

They didn't stop until they were outside, the air thick with tension. Isabel turned to Lucía, her hands gripping her shoulders. "What was that?" she demanded, her voice a mix of fear and disbelief.

Lucía didn't answer, her eyes brimming with unshed tears as she clutched her notebook tightly.

Isabel exhaled shakily, pulling Lucía into a fierce embrace. "We're going to be okay," she whispered, though her own voice wavered. "We'll figure this out. Together."

Lucía nodded against her shoulder, her silent tears soaking into Isabel's dress.

The world outside the convent was far more complicated—and far more dangerous—than either of them had imagined.

A New Beginning

After several days of searching, Isabel and Lucía finally found a place that fit their modest budget—a small but welcoming apartment on the edge of the city. The space had a lived-in charm, with creaky wooden floors and large windows that let in plenty of sunlight. It wasn't much, but it felt like a beginning. They never spoke to Maria about the unsettling incident with the abusive landlord, both silently agreeing to leave it in the past.

Back at the shelter, they shared their news with Maria over steaming cups of tea at the kitchen table.

"That's wonderful," Maria said, her eyes lighting up. "When do you move in?"

"Tomorrow," Isabel replied, her tone a mix of relief and excitement. "The landlord even offered to help us with a few pieces of furniture."

Maria's smile softened with genuine warmth. "You've come so far in such a short time. I hope you both know how proud you should be of yourselves."

Lucía pulled out her notebook, scribbling a note with careful strokes before passing it across the table to Maria.

Thank you for everything.

Maria read the words and reached out, clasping Lucía's hand between her own. "You're so welcome. But you don't have to thank me. You did this yourselves. Just remember—you're never truly alone. Not here, not anywhere."

That night, as they settled into their small shared room for the last time, Isabel lay back on her cot, staring at the ceiling. The day's events replayed in her mind, blending excitement with nervous anticipation.

"Lucía," she said softly, turning her head toward the faint outline of her companion illuminated by the moonlight. "We did it. Our first real step."

Lucía looked up from her notebook, her face calm but her eyes glowing with determination. She turned the page toward Isabel, the words clear in the moonlight:

The world is big. But we're bigger together.

Isabel felt a lump rise in her throat, her heart swelling with pride and gratitude. "Yes, we are," she said quietly, her voice brimming with affection. She leaned over, switching off the small bedside lamp, plunging the room into a comforting darkness.

Tomorrow will bring new challenges, new discoveries, and perhaps new fears. But for now, they rested, side by side, their hearts quietly brimming with the strength of their shared journey.

6

Late Shadows

Lucía sat alone in the small apartment, the notebook open on the table in front of her. Outside, the city buzzed with life—cars honking in the distance, faint laughter spilling out from the bar across the street. Neon lights from a nearby sign pulsed intermittently, casting fractured patterns across the walls. The flickering colors felt chaotic, out of place in the otherwise pristine order of the room.

She glanced at the clock on the wall. **10:47 p.m.**

Isabel was late. Again.

Lucía's fingers tightened around her pen, her unease settling like a stone in her chest. This was the third time this week. She tried to focus on the list she had been writing—groceries, laundry, a new recipe to try—but the pen hovered uselessly above the page. No matter how hard she tried to concentrate, her thoughts kept drifting to Isabel.

Where was she?

The sound of keys rattling at the door snapped Lucía's head up. Her heart quickened, but she kept her expression neutral, her grip firm on the pen.

The door creaked open, and Isabel stepped inside. Her cheeks were flushed, her hair slightly tousled, and her coat hung loosely from one shoulder. She kicked off her shoes without looking up, her movements hurried, almost distracted.

"Sorry I'm late," Isabel said, her voice light but strained. She dropped her bag by the couch and ran a hand through her hair, still avoiding Lucía's gaze.

Lucía's pen moved quickly across the page. She held up the notebook: **"You said you'd be back by nine."**

"I know," Isabel replied, her tone dismissive as she shrugged out of her coat. "Robert and I stayed late to clean up. The place was a mess."

Lucía didn't miss the way Isabel's voice softened slightly when she said his name. She wrote again, her strokes sharp and deliberate: **"This keeps happening. You didn't even call."**

Isabel sighed, exasperated. She flopped onto the couch, her bag still at her feet. "I didn't think I needed to, Lucía. I'm an adult. I can take care of myself."

Lucía's lips pressed into a thin line. Her pen scratched furiously across the page: **"It's not about you being an adult. It's about respect."**

"Respect?" Isabel's voice rose, her frustration bubbling to the surface. She sat up straighter, her eyes finally meeting Lucía's. "Lucía, I'm working hard to keep us afloat. If I stay late or go out, it's not because I'm disrespecting you—it's because I'm doing what needs to be done."

Lucía's eyes narrowed. She stared at Isabel for a long moment before closing her notebook with a sharp snap. The sound echoed in the room, cutting through the tense silence like a whip.

For a moment, neither of them spoke. The air seemed to thicken, heavy and oppressive. Isabel shifted uncomfortably, a faint prickling sensation crawling up her spine.

"Lucía..." Isabel began, her voice faltering as her sister's gaze bore into her.

The lights flickered suddenly, the faint hum of electricity filling the silence. Isabel's eyes darted to the overhead bulb, then back to Lucía, her unease growing.

"Lucía," Isabel said again, more firmly this time, though her voice trembled slightly. "Stop."

The tension in the room broke as quickly as it had come. The lights steadied, and the strange weight in the air dissipated. Lucía stood abruptly, her movements stiff, and turned her back to Isabel.

"I'm sorry," Isabel said softly, her earlier frustration fading into guilt. "I'll call next time, okay? I promise."

Lucía didn't respond. She picked up her notebook and clutched it tightly to her chest as she walked to her room. The door closed behind her with a quiet but resolute click.

A Whispered Prayer

Lucía sat cross-legged on her bed, the notebook resting open on her lap. The room was dim, lit only by the faint glow of the streetlamp filtering through the curtains. The muffled sounds of the city outside seemed far away, irrelevant against the storm of emotions swirling in her chest.

She stared at the blank page in front of her, her pen trembling in her hand. The silence in the room was heavy, pressing down on her like a weight she couldn't lift.

Her mind raced back to the argument with Isabel. The flush of Isabel's cheeks, the defensiveness in her tone, the way she'd avoided Lucía's eyes—all of it replayed over and over like a loop she couldn't stop.

Her hands clenched around the pen, frustration surging. She wanted to scream, to cry, to demand answers, but no sound would ever come. Instead, the words she couldn't speak formed in her mind, sharp and pleading.

God, what am I supposed to do?

Her grip on the pen tightened as her thoughts tumbled forward, unchecked. **She's slipping away, Lord. I can feel it. She's being pulled into a world that's louder, brighter, and so far from You. I don't know how to bring her back. I don't even know if I can.**

Her chest tightened, and tears blurred her vision. She let the pen fall onto the page, her hands covering her face as silent sobs wracked her body.

Why did You choose me for this? she thought, the question reverberating in her mind. **I'm not strong enough. I don't know how to guide her. I can barely understand what You're asking of me. How am I supposed to save her when I don't even know if I'm doing this right?**

The air in the room shifted suddenly.

Lucía froze, her breath catching. The faint glow from the streetlamp dimmed, the shadows in the corners of the room deepening as if they were alive. Even the distant hum of the city seemed to fade, leaving only the sound of her heartbeat pounding in her ears.

Her hand moved toward the pen, almost without thinking. The moment her fingers curled around it, the stillness grew heavier, as though the very room was holding its breath.

The pen began to glide across the page.

Lucía's hand trembled, but it wasn't her doing. The strokes were deliberate, steady, and unyielding. She felt as if something far greater than herself had taken over, guiding her hand with a purpose she couldn't comprehend.

When the pen stilled, she stared down at the page.

"RETURN."

Her breath hitched.

The word seemed to pulse faintly in the dim light, bold and unshakable. She reached out hesitantly, her fingers brushing over the letters. They felt warm, almost alive, as though imbued with a presence she couldn't name.

The Silent Monologue

Lucía clutched the notebook to her chest, her tears falling freely now. Her thoughts poured out, each one a silent cry into the void.

Why this word? Why now? Is this what You're asking of me? To return? To bring her back with me? I don't understand, Lord. What if she won't come? What if I can't do this? What if I fail?

Her body shook with the weight of her fears. **You see everything, don't You? You see how she's changing. How she's drawn to Robert, to the world outside. How she's drifting further from You.**

Her fingers tightened around the notebook, as though it could anchor her. **Is that why You've given me this? Because I can see it? Because I'm the only one who can stop it? But I don't know how, Lord. I don't know how to lead her. I don't know how to do this without losing her completely.**

Her tears fell onto the page, smudging the ink slightly, but the word remained clear, steady, and resolute.

If this is Your will, show me how. Teach me. Help me find the strength to bring her back—not just to the convent, but to You. Please, Lord. Don't let me fail her.

The air shifted again, this time lighter, though no less powerful. Lucía opened her eyes, her breath coming in short gasps.

The word **RETURN** seemed to glow faintly, its presence filling the room. For the first time, the weight in her chest began to ease, replaced by a calm that felt almost unnatural.

She exhaled slowly, her trembling hands smoothing over the page. Her doubts remained, but there was something else now, too. A quiet knowing. A steady rhythm that pulsed alongside her heartbeat.

The Resolve

Lucía closed the notebook slowly, pressing it to her chest once more. Sliding it beneath her pillow, she lay back against the mattress, her eyes fixed on the faint patterns of light shifting across the ceiling.

RETURN.

The word echoed in her mind, no longer just an instruction but a promise.

In the other room, she could faintly hear Isabel moving about, her footsteps soft against the floorboards. The sound felt distant, as though part of a world Lucía no longer belonged to.

Far away, the city continued its restless hum, but Lucía remained still, her heart steadier now. The task ahead loomed large, but for the first time, she felt the smallest glimmer of certainty.

This wasn't just her choice. It was her calling.

7

Shadows of Truth

The air in the apartment felt heavier than usual, as if the walls themselves were listening. Lucía sat at the small kitchen table, her notebook open in front of her. The faint hum of the refrigerator was the only sound breaking the silence. She tapped her pen against the page, her thoughts swirling.

She glanced toward the clock. Isabel would be home soon. Her heart clenched at the thought of their earlier argument, the sharpness of Isabel's voice still echoing in her mind. The words **"I'm going back to the convent"** had been met with disbelief, anger, and a pain Lucía hadn't anticipated. She knew Isabel wouldn't accept it easily, but she hadn't expected her to be so adamant, so unwilling to even consider the possibility.

Lucía's pen hovered above the page. She stared at the word she had written last night, **RETURN,** bold and unwavering. Beneath it, her hand moved almost instinctively, forming another word: **REVEAL.** She stared at the letters, her pulse quickening. They felt significant, though she didn't fully understand why.

The sound of the key turning in the lock pulled her from her thoughts. She closed the notebook quickly, sliding it toward the edge of the table as Isabel walked in.

"Hey," Isabel said, her tone casual, though there was a weariness in her voice. She dropped her bag by the door and kicked off her shoes. "I don't want to fight anymore, okay? Let's just... drop it."

Lucía nodded but didn't reach for her notebook. Instead, she gestured toward the small teapot on the stove, silently offering to pour her a cup.

Isabel shook her head, brushing a hand through her hair. "Thanks, but I'm fine." She hesitated, her eyes flickering to the notebook. "I mean it, Lucía. We've worked too hard to build this life. Going back... it doesn't make sense. You know that, right?"

Lucía didn't respond, her expression calm but unreadable. She reached for her pen and wrote slowly, deliberately: **"Do you trust me?"**

Isabel blinked, her brow furrowing. "Of course I do."

Lucía slid the notebook across the table, pointing to the word **RETURN.** Her pen moved again, forming another question: **"Do you trust Him?"**

Isabel's lips parted slightly, a flicker of something—doubt, frustration, fear—crossing her face. She stepped back, her arms crossing over her chest. "This isn't about trust, Lucía. It's about reality. About the life we've built here. God doesn't expect us to just walk away from that, does He?"

Lucía tilted her head, her gaze steady. Her pen scratched against the page again: **"Maybe He does."**

Isabel let out a bitter laugh, shaking her head. "You don't get it. You've always been the strong one, the faithful one. But me? I'm different. I've found something here, Lucía. Something real."

Lucía's pen paused, her eyes narrowing slightly. She wrote quickly, her strokes sharp: **"Is it Robert?"**

The question hung in the air like a weight. Isabel froze, her cheeks flushing. "What? No. This isn't about him."

Lucía didn't look away. She underlined his name, her expression quiet but insistent.

"I said it's not about him!" Isabel snapped, her voice rising. "Why does everything have to come back to Robert?"

Lucía leaned forward, her pen moving deliberately: **"Because you're not being honest."**

Isabel's breath hitched. She stepped back, her hands shaking slightly. "I'm being honest," she said, but her voice cracked, betraying her. "I... I just don't know if I can go back to that life. It's suffocating, Lucía. It's... it's not who I am anymore."

Lucía's gaze softened, and she reached across the table, taking Isabel's hand in hers. Her next words were slow, almost tender: **"Maybe it's not about who you were. Maybe it's about who you're meant to be."**

Isabel's shoulders sagged, her defenses crumbling. She sank into the chair across from Lucía, her face buried in her hands. "You don't understand," she whispered, her voice muffled. "I feel... torn. Like I'm caught between two worlds, and no matter which one I choose, I'm going to lose something important."

Lucía squeezed her hand gently, her expression full of quiet compassion. She didn't write anything this time, letting the silence speak for her.

After a long moment, Isabel exhaled shakily, wiping at her eyes. "Fine," she murmured, her voice barely audible. "I'll go with you. But I'm not promising to stay."

Lucía nodded, her smile small but genuine.

The next day, as Isabel left for work, Lucía remained in the apartment, her thoughts heavy. She felt the shift before it happened, a strange tightening in the air. Her hand moved toward the notebook, and the pen glided across the page almost of its own accord. When she looked down, the word **REVEAL** stared back at her, bold and unyielding.

At the café, Isabel was clearing tables when the news broke. One of her coworkers called her over, their face pale.

"Isabel, you need to see this."

The TV above the counter displayed a breaking news alert. A car accident. Isabel's heart stopped as she recognized the license plate of the crumpled sedan being towed from the scene.

"No," she whispered, her hands trembling.

"It's Robert," her coworker said gently. "They just said he's at Mercy General. It doesn't look good."

Without a word, Isabel grabbed her bag and ran out the door.

The hospital was a blur of sterile lights and hushed voices. Isabel rushed to the reception desk, her breath coming in short, panicked gasps. "I'm here for Robert," she managed, her voice shaking.

The nurse gave her a sympathetic look. "I'm sorry, but he passed away shortly after arriving." She hesitated, then added, "His wife is over there with the children, if you'd like to speak with her."

The words hit Isabel like a blow. **His wife?**

She turned slowly, her eyes falling on a woman sitting in the corner of the waiting room. The woman held two small children close, her face streaked with tears.

Time seemed to stop. Isabel stood frozen, her breath caught in her chest as the nurse's words echoed in her mind. Her eyes locked on the woman sitting in the corner of the waiting room, her arms wrapped protectively around two children. The woman's shoulders shook with quiet sobs, her face pale and streaked with tears.

Each step Isabel took toward her felt heavier than the last. The ground seemed to shift beneath her, as though her body were protesting the weight of the truth she was about to confront.

The woman looked up as Isabel approached, her red-rimmed eyes meeting Isabel's. For a moment, neither of them spoke. The woman's lips quivered as she drew the children closer.

"Did you know my husband?" she asked softly, her voice brittle and raw.

Isabel's mouth felt dry, her heart pounding so loudly she could barely hear herself. "I... I worked with him," she managed, the words falling flat. She hesitated, then added, "My condolences."

The woman nodded faintly, her grip on her children tightening. "Thank you," she whispered, her voice cracking on the word.

Isabel didn't move. Her eyes flicked to the children, their small faces tucked into their mother's side, oblivious to the weight of the moment. She opened her mouth, then closed it again, unsure how to ask the questions clawing at her chest.

"He spoke about you sometimes," Isabel said finally, her voice trembling. "About his family. He seemed so proud of you all."

The woman blinked at her, fresh tears brimming in her eyes. "He was a good father," she murmured. "At least, he tried to be. It wasn't always easy, with him working so much. But he loved these two more than anything." She smoothed a hand over her daughter's hair, her touch trembling.

Isabel's stomach twisted. "He worked late a lot," she said cautiously, her words heavy with unspoken meaning.

"Yes," the woman said, her lips pressing into a thin line. "Too much, really. There were nights I barely saw him. He'd call and say he was swamped at the café, that he'd be home late. He always sounded so tired..." Her voice faltered, a shadow crossing her face.

Isabel swallowed hard, the knot in her throat tightening. "He... called often?"

The woman nodded. "He tried to, at least. Said he didn't want me to worry. But you know how it is—sometimes I'd wake up and he'd already be gone. I told myself it was just part of his job, that he was doing it all for us." Her voice trembled, a faint bitterness creeping in. "Now... I don't know what to think."

Isabel's breath hitched. She forced herself to keep her expression neutral, though her heart threatened to break through her ribs. "What do you mean?"

The woman's eyes met hers again, sharp and searching. "There were moments," she admitted, her words hesitant, as though she feared them. "Moments when things didn't add up. A receipt for a place he shouldn't have been. A missed call he didn't explain. I told myself it didn't matter, that I was imagining things. But now..." She shook her head, her voice breaking. "Now I'll never know, will I?"

Isabel's chest ached, guilt and grief colliding in a storm she could barely contain. Her mind raced, fragments of memories flashing before her—the quiet moments she'd shared with Robert, the way his hand lingered too long, the way he looked at her when no one else was around.

"He was good at making people feel seen," Isabel said softly, her words careful.

The woman let out a sharp, bitter laugh. "That he was," she said, her tone cutting. "He could charm anyone, couldn't he? Even when things were falling apart, he'd walk into the room and make you believe everything was fine. It's what I fell in love with. And, I guess... what I couldn't see past." Her voice cracked, and she turned her face away, burying it in her hands.

Isabel hesitated, the weight of her next words pressing heavily on her chest. "Did you ever ask him?" she said quietly.

The woman's shoulders tensed. "No," she whispered. "I didn't want to hear the answer. I thought it would break me." She wiped her tears quickly, as if ashamed of them. "Now I wish I had."

Isabel stood there, her legs trembling beneath her. She wanted to say something, to offer comfort, but the words caught in her throat. She could only nod, her heart breaking under the weight of the truth.

The woman looked up again, her gaze softening slightly. "You said you worked with him?"

Isabel nodded slowly. "Yes," she said, her voice barely audible.

"Did he seem happy?" the woman asked, her voice trembling.

The question pierced through Isabel like a blade. She hesitated, her mind racing. "I think... he was searching for something," she said finally, her words measured.

The woman stared at her for a long moment, then gave a small, sad nod. "I guess we all are," she murmured, pulling her children closer.

Isabel lingered for a moment longer, her body heavy with the weight of all the things she couldn't say. She offered the woman a faint, trembling smile. "I'm so sorry for your loss," she said again, her voice breaking.

"Thank you," the woman whispered.

As Isabel turned to leave, her legs felt unsteady, as if they might give out beneath her. The fluorescent lights above blurred, the room spinning faintly around her. Outside, the cold air hit her face like a slap, but it did nothing to clear the storm in her chest.

Her mind raced, the pieces of Robert's life—his charm, his secrets, his lies—falling into place with devastating clarity. She thought she had known him. She thought she had mattered to him.

But now, standing under the unforgiving glare of the hospital lights, Isabel realized the truth. She had been a piece of his puzzle, just like everyone else.

And she hated him for it.

Isabel lingered for a moment, then turned and walked away, her heart shattering.

The apartment felt colder than usual when Isabel stepped inside. She closed the door quietly, her movements slow and deliberate. Lucía was seated at the kitchen table, her notebook open, her pen moving in small, precise strokes. The faint glow from the lamp cast a warm light across her face, but Isabel felt none of its comfort.

Lucía glanced up, her brow furrowing as she took in Isabel's pale complexion and trembling hands. She wrote quickly, sliding the notebook across the table.

"What happened?"

Isabel hesitated, standing frozen in the doorway. The words clawed at her throat, desperate to be said, but her voice wouldn't come. Her knees buckled slightly as she moved to the chair across from Lucía, sinking into it with a heaviness that made the air between them feel oppressive.

"I don't know how to say this," Isabel began, her voice cracking. She pressed her hands against her temples, her fingers trembling. "Robert... he... he's gone."

Lucía's pen stilled. She tilted her head slightly, her expression calm but searching, as if waiting for Isabel to continue.

"He had an accident," Isabel said, her words tumbling out in a rush. "He was driving late last night... and... and he didn't make it." Her voice broke on the last word, and she buried her face in her hands, muffling the sob that escaped her.

Lucía's pen moved again, her strokes slow and deliberate. **"I'm so sorry, Isabel. Were you close?"**

Isabel let out a bitter laugh, lifting her head to meet her sister's gaze. "Close?" she repeated, the word dripping with irony. "I thought I knew him, Lucía. I thought he was... something else.

Someone else. But he had a whole life I didn't know about. A wife. Kids." She let the words hang in the air, each one cutting deeper.

Lucía's pen moved with precision: **"That must be so painful."**

"Painful doesn't even begin to cover it," Isabel snapped, though her anger wasn't directed at Lucía. She leaned back in the chair, her eyes red and swollen. "I trusted him. I believed everything he told me. And now I find out he was lying to me—lying to everyone. What does that make me?"

Lucía tilted her head, her pen moving quickly: **"It makes you human. It doesn't make you wrong for trusting him."**

Isabel's breath hitched, her hands clenching into fists. "I should've known. The late nights, the vague excuses, the way he'd brush off questions... It was all there, wasn't it? And I ignored it because I... because I..." Her voice trailed off, her chest heaving as she tried to suppress the flood of emotions.

Lucía's pen hovered over the page, then moved again: **"Because you cared about him."**

Isabel nodded, her lips trembling. "And look where that got me." She paused, a sudden thought creeping into her mind, unbidden and unwanted. She stared at Lucía, the question forming before she could stop it.

Could Lucía have had something to do with this?

The thought was absurd, ridiculous—but it lingered for a heartbeat longer than it should have. The way Lucía always seemed to know more than she let on, the subtle shifts in her demeanor when things happened around them... Isabel shook her head sharply, as if trying to physically dislodge the idea.

No. Lucía wouldn't—couldn't.

"What are you thinking?" Lucía's pen moved with surprising speed.

Isabel flinched slightly, her cheeks flushing. "Nothing," she said quickly. "It's nothing."

Lucía narrowed her eyes but didn't press. Instead, she reached across the table, placing her hand over Isabel's. Her touch was firm, grounding, as if to silently say: I'm here.

Isabel exhaled shakily, her resolve crumbling under her sister's steady presence. "I don't know how to move past this," she admitted, her voice barely above a whisper. "I don't even know who I am anymore."

Lucía wrote again: **"You're my sister. You're stronger than you think."**

The simplicity of the words made Isabel's eyes well up again. She looked away quickly, her gaze falling to her bag on the floor. "I need to lie down," she muttered, standing abruptly.

Lucía didn't try to stop her, only nodding as Isabel disappeared into her room.

Inside her room, Isabel closed the door and leaned against it, her chest heaving as if she had been holding her breath for hours. Her eyes flicked to the nightstand, where the envelope Robert had given her sat like a specter of the life she thought she had.

She reached for it slowly, her hands trembling as she unfolded the paper inside. The letter stared back at her, their meaning undeniable. Her stomach churned, the nausea rising again, but she swallowed it down.

"What am I supposed to do now?" she whispered, her voice trembling.

Her mind raced, fragments of memories flashing before her—Robert's smile, his touch, the way he'd made her feel like she was the only one who mattered. She crumpled the paper in her hands, pressing it against her forehead as if she could erase everything it represented.

The next few days passed in a blur of exhaustion and anxiety. Isabel forced herself to go to work, though each step felt like wading through quicksand. Her coworkers gave her space, their concerned glances only heightened her sense of isolation.

During breaks, she sat alone in the corner of the café, cradling a cup of coffee she couldn't bring herself to drink. The nausea came in waves, growing stronger with each passing day.

One afternoon, as she delivered an order to a table, dizziness hit her like a freight train. She barely made it to the bathroom before her stomach heaved violently.

When she emerged, pale and unsteady, her boss was waiting for her near the door. His expression was firm but not unkind.

"Isabel, you don't look well," he said.

"I'm fine," she said weakly, though the lie was transparent.

He shook his head. "Take a few days off. Rest. Get better." His voice softened slightly, his eyes narrowing as he added, "Do what you need to do, okay?"

The weight of his implication wasn't lost on her. Her face flushed, and she nodded stiffly, mumbling a quiet "Thank you" before grabbing her things and leaving.

The apartment was dim when Isabel entered, her steps slow and deliberate. She dropped her bag by the door, pausing to lean against the frame, her breath shallow. Lucía was in the living room, her notebook open on her lap, pen moving in steady strokes.

Isabel barely glanced at her sister as she shuffled past, muttering, "I'm going to lie down."

Lucía didn't reply. Her pen continued its movements, scratching across the page with quiet precision. Isabel didn't notice the way her sister's hand slowed, the way her eyes darkened, focused on something unseen.

Once Isabel's door clicked shut, the air in the apartment seemed to change. A stillness crept in, heavy and tangible, like the moment before a storm. Lucía's pen paused, her hand trembling slightly as a strange heat bloomed in her chest.

She stared at the words she had just written:

"She's not ready yet."

Lucía frowned, her brow furrowing. The words felt foreign, as if someone else had guided her hand. She turned the notebook toward herself, running her fingers over the letters. They seemed to shimmer faintly under the dim light, pulsing with an energy she couldn't name.

Her heart quickened. She looked toward Isabel's closed door, a flicker of something—concern? Fear? rising in her chest. The urge to stand, to intervene, washed over her, but she forced herself to stay seated.

Instead, she picked up her pen again, her hand trembling as it hovered over the page. Her thoughts spiraled, chaotic and untethered, but a single phrase crystallized in her mind. She didn't write it down; she didn't need to.

"She must choose."

The words echoed in her chest, a low hum that seemed to reverberate through the apartment. Lucía closed the notebook quickly, pressing it against her heart as she leaned back in the chair, her breaths shallow.

In the other room, Isabel stirred in her bed, her sleep restless. She murmured softly, incoherent words tumbling from her lips as she turned onto her side. The faintest shadow crossed her face, unnoticed in the dim light.

Lucía exhaled, her grip on the notebook tightening.

She didn't know how she knew it, but she was certain of one thing:

Isabel's path wasn't hers to dictate. But the steps leading to it? Those were.

8

Breaking Point

The air in the apartment felt heavy, as if even the walls held their breath. Isabel paced the small kitchen, her arms crossed tightly over her chest. Her footsteps echoed against the tiles, the sharp sound grating against Lucía's quiet presence.

Lucía sat at the table, her notebook open, her pen poised but unmoving. She watched her sister with calm, observant eyes, her expression serene despite the storm raging in the room.

"Stop looking at me like that!" Isabel snapped, her voice cutting through the silence. She turned to face Lucía, her cheeks flushed with frustration. "You don't understand what I'm going through. You can't possibly understand."

Lucía tilted her head slightly, her pen finally moving. She slid the notebook across the table. **"You don't think I see you?"**

Isabel let out a bitter laugh, throwing her hands up in exasperation. "See me? What does that even mean, Lucía? You sit there calm and silent, while my whole life is falling apart. How is that supposed to help?"

Lucía's hand moved again, her strokes deliberate. **"You're not alone."**

"Not alone?" Isabel's voice cracked, her anger giving way to a flood of emotion. "I've never felt more alone in my entire life.

Robert's gone. My body feels like it's betraying me. And you—" She pointed an accusatory finger at Lucía. "You just sit there, scribbling in that damn notebook, like it's all some kind of puzzle you're trying to solve."

Lucía stood slowly, her movements deliberate. She closed the notebook and held it to her chest, her gaze steadily as she walked toward Isabel. When she stopped a few feet away, she opened the notebook again, her hand trembling slightly as she wrote a single word.

She turned the notebook around and held it up for Isabel to see: **"LEUKEMIA."**

Isabel froze, the word slamming into her like a physical blow. Her mouth opened, but no sound came out. She staggered back a step, her hand clutching the edge of the counter for support.

"No," she whispered, her voice barely audible. "No, that's not... how could you..." Her words trailed off as tears spilled down her cheeks.

Lucía stepped closer, her movements slow and deliberate. She reached out, placing a hand gently on Isabel's shoulder.

"How do you know?" Isabel asked, her voice trembling. Her eyes searched Lucía's face for answers, for some kind of explanation. "I never told you."

Lucía's expression softened. She wrote carefully, her strokes steady despite the tremor in her hand: **"I just know."**

Isabel's knees buckled, and she sank to the floor, her body wracked with sobs. "It's not fair," she choked out. "I didn't ask for this. Any of it."

Lucía knelt beside her, wrapping her arms around her sister's trembling frame. She held her tightly, her silence filled with a depth of understanding that words could never convey.

For a long time, they stayed like that, the only sound in the room Isabel's broken cries. When her sobs finally subsided, she pulled away slightly, her face pale and streaked with tears.

"What am I supposed to do?" Isabel whispered, her voice small and fragile.

Lucía picked up the notebook again, her pen moving with quiet certainty: **"You already know."**

Isabel's breath hitched. She shook her head, her tears starting anew. "I can't, Lucía. I can't go back. Not like this."

Lucía tilted her head, her gaze unwavering. She wrote another line, her strokes precise: **"You're stronger than you think."**

"I'm not," Isabel said, shaking her head fiercely. "I've made so many mistakes. I've strayed so far... How could He ever want me back?"

Lucía cupped Isabel's face in her hands, forcing her to meet her gaze. Her eyes shone with a quiet intensity, as if trying to will the truth into her sister's heart. She wrote slowly this time, the letters deliberate: **"He's never stopped wanting you."**

Isabel broke into fresh sobs, burying her face in her hands. The weight of Lucía's words—of their truth—pressed down on her, but they also offered the faintest glimmer of hope.

In the days that followed, the apartment seemed to exhale in the quiet. The once faint hum of the refrigerator and the muted sounds of the city outside now felt amplified, filling the void where conversations had once been. Isabel moved through her routines like a shadow, her thoughts tangled and heavy. She folded laundry with trembling hands, her mind far away. She washed dishes without noticing the water growing cold.

The envelope, tucked in the back of her nightstand, might as well have been a weight on her chest. She avoided looking at it, but she couldn't escape its presence. The word **RETURN** whispered in her mind, insistent and unrelenting, but the thought of going back to the convent felt like stepping off a ledge she couldn't see the bottom of.

Lucía, however, had already begun preparing. She cleaned with unusual precision, folding linens, scrubbing the stove, and straightening their modest bookshelf. Her actions were deliberate, as though she were organizing not just their space but their lives for what was to come. She didn't speak of it, but the message was clear: they would be leaving soon.

One afternoon, as the weak winter sunlight filtered through the curtains, Isabel sat at the kitchen table. A cup of tea rested in front of her, untouched, its steam curling lazily into the air. Across from her, Lucía sat with her notebook, her pen resting against the blank page.

The silence stretched between them, thick with unspoken words. Finally, Isabel broke it. "Why do you believe so easily?" Her voice was barely above a whisper, yet it carried the weight of all her doubts, her fears, her exhaustion.

Lucía's pen moved across the page with steady strokes. She turned the notebook toward Isabel: **"Because I've seen."**

Isabel frowned, her brow furrowing deeply. "Seen what?" she pressed, her voice sharper now, tinged with desperation.

Lucía hesitated, her pen poised above the page. She seemed to choose her next words carefully, each stroke deliberates as she wrote: **"Him."**

The word landed like a stone in Isabel's chest. She stared at her sister, her breath catching in her throat. "What do you mean? What did you see?"

Lucía didn't look away. Her eyes held a quiet certainty, steady and unshakable, that sent a shiver through Isabel. She wrote again, slowly this time: **"I saw His light. His love. His call."**

Isabel shook her head, her hand gripping the edge of the table as though it might keep her grounded. "How can you be so sure? How do you know it wasn't... I don't know... a dream, or your imagination?"

Lucía's expression softened, her pen moving once more: **"Because it changed me."**

Isabel's voice broke as she asked, "And what if I'm too broken to hear Him? What if I've strayed too far?"

Lucía reached across the table, her hand resting gently over Isabel's. Her touch was warm, grounding, as if to say: **I'm here. You're not alone.** She wrote again: **"You're not too far. You've never been too far."**

Tears welled in Isabel's eyes. She turned her face away, trying to hide her vulnerability, but the weight of her sister's unwavering faith was too much. "You make it sound so simple," she whispered.

Lucía squeezed her hand gently, then wrote: **"It's not simple. But it's clear."**

The word **RETURN** pulsed in Isabel's mind, brighter now, like a beacon she couldn't ignore. She pressed her free hand to her chest, her tears spilling over. "I'm scared, Lucía," she admitted, her voice breaking. "What if I can't do this? What if I fail again?"

Lucía stood, moving around the table to kneel beside her sister. She cupped Isabel's face in her hands, her touch firm yet tender, and looked into her tear-filled eyes. Her pen moved carefully: **"You don't have to be perfect. You just have to trust."**

Isabel sobbed openly now, the sound raw and guttural, as though years of pain and fear were spilling out all at once. Lucía held her, her arms wrapping around her trembling frame, offering comfort without words.

For a long time, they stayed like that, the air around them heavy with emotion. When Isabel finally pulled back, her face was streaked with tears, but her breathing was steadier. "Do you really think He still wants me?" she asked, her voice small and fragile.

Lucía didn't hesitate. She wrote boldly: **"He's always wanted you."**

Isabel closed her eyes, the weight of those words settled into her heart. The word **RETURN** blazed in her mind, no longer a whisper but a command she couldn't ignore.

9

Walking the Path

The sunlight filtered weakly through the curtains, casting muted patterns on the kitchen floor. The apartment was too quiet, the kind of silence that pressed down like a weight. Isabel sat at the table, her hands wrapped around a mug of tea she hadn't touched. Across from her, Lucía scribbled something in her notebook, the faint scratch of her pen the only sound in the room.

Isabel glanced up, her face drawn and pale. "You're writing again," she said, her voice brittle. "What is it this time? Another cryptic note about how I should 'listen to Him' or 'trust the path'?"

Lucía looked up, her expression calm as she turned the notebook toward Isabel. **"You're not listening to yourself, either."**

Isabel frowned, her fingers tightening around the mug. "What's that supposed to mean?"

Lucía wrote carefully: **"You're fighting what you already know."**

Isabel laughed bitterly, the sound sharp and hollow. "Oh, that's rich. Enlighten me, Lucía. What exactly do I know?"

Lucía's gaze didn't waver. She wrote: **"That you can't keep running."**

Isabel slammed the mug down, the tea sloshing over the edge. "Running? From what? From Him? From this so-called path you keep talking about?" She leaned forward, her voice rising. "You don't know what I've been through, Lucía. You don't know what I've done."

Lucía's pen moved swiftly: **"Then tell me."**

Isabel froze, her chest heaving as she stared at her sister. The challenge in Lucía's calm demeanor was unbearable. She pushed back her chair and began pacing, her hands tangling in her hair. "You don't want to know. You think you do, but you don't."

Lucía stood, her notebook still in hand. She followed Isabel's frantic movements with steady eyes. **"Try me,"** she wrote, holding the notebook up like a mirror.

Isabel stopped, her back to Lucía. Her shoulders slumped, and for a long moment, she said nothing. When she finally turned, her eyes glistened with unshed tears. "Fine. You want the truth? Here it is: I loved him. Robert. I thought he loved me, too. I thought... I thought he saw me."

Lucía remained silent, waiting.

"And I gave him everything," Isabel continued, her voice trembling. "I let him into parts of myself I thought were sacred. I broke every vow I ever made, every promise I swore to keep. And now..." She laughed bitterly, the sound choking in her throat. "Now, I can't even look at myself, let alone face God."

Lucía stepped closer, her movements deliberate. She wrote with steady hands: **"You loved. You made mistakes. That doesn't mean you're lost."**

Isabel's tears spilled over. "Doesn't it? I can't go back, Lucía. I can't stand in that chapel and pretend to be worthy of Him after what I've done"

Lucía tilted her head, her pen moving again: **"Faith isn't pretending. It's trying."**

Isabel let out a sob, sinking into the chair. "You make it sound so simple."

Lucía sat beside her, setting the notebook down. She reached out, taking Isabel's trembling hands in hers. Her touch was firm but gentle, grounding. She wrote slowly, her strokes deliberate: **"God shows us the path, but it's up to us to walk it."**

Isabel shook her head, her tears falling freely. "I don't even know where the path is anymore."

Lucía picked up the pen again, her movements steady: **"Let's Walk it together. He will show you the way."**

Isabel stared at her sister, the words sinking like a balm to her fractured soul. For the first time, she allowed herself to feel the faintest glimmer of hope.

In the days that followed, the apartment hummed with the quiet rhythm of preparation. Lucía moved through the space with purpose, her actions methodical and deliberate. She folded clothes with the precision of someone arranging not just fabric, but their future. Each corner of the apartment was cleaned as though she were erasing the remnants of a life left in the margins, making way for something new.

Isabel, however, moved like a ghost. Her steps were slow, her gaze distant, her hands trembling as she picked up objects only to set them down again. Packing felt surreal, as though she were dismantling not just their home but the fragile structure of her identity. The envelope from Robert remained hidden in her suitcase, its presence a quiet reminder of all she had tried to suppress.

One afternoon, sunlight poured through the window, casting golden streaks across the floor. Isabel sat cross-legged on the rug, a framed photograph of her and Lucía as children resting in her lap. Her fingertips traced the edges of the frame, her expression faraway.

"Do you ever wonder," Isabel began softly, her voice barely breaking the stillness, "if we'd have been better off staying there?"

Lucía paused, a half-folded shirt in her hands. She glanced at Isabel, her head tilting slightly as though considering the weight of the question. Setting the shirt aside, she picked up her notebook and wrote: **"We were meant to leave. And now we're meant to go back."**

Isabel let out a quiet scoff, setting the frame aside as she pulled her knees to her chest. "You're so sure of everything. I wish I could be like that."

Lucía didn't respond right away. She set the notebook down and watched Isabel for a long moment, her calm gaze unwavering. Finally, she picked up her pen and wrote: **"Tell me what you're carrying."**

Isabel let out a bitter laugh, shaking her head. "What's the point? You'll just say it doesn't matter. That God forgives everything if you ask Him nicely enough."

Lucía tilted her head slightly and wrote: **"You've been holding this alone for too long. Let me help."**

Isabel's jaw tightened, her hands clenching into fists on her lap. "You don't understand, Lucía. You can't understand."

Lucía slid the notebook toward her, her strokes deliberate: **"Help me understand."**

Isabel stared at the page, the challenge in Lucía's quiet persistence slicing through her defenses. Her shoulders sagged, and she pressed her hands to her face. "Fine. You want to know? I'll tell you. I let him in—Robert. I thought he loved me. I thought he saw me for who I was, and I..." Her voice broke, and she drew a shaky breath. "I gave him everything. Everything I thought I'd saved for God."

Lucía remained still, her pen hovering above the page. Finally, she wrote: **"You gave him your heart."**

Isabel nodded miserably. "And what did I get in return? Lies. Pain. He wasn't who I thought he was, and now he's gone. And I—" She stopped, her voice cracking. "I can't go back, Lucía. Not after this. I can't stand in that chapel and pretend to be worthy of Him. Not after I betrayed Him."

Isabel shook her head, tears streaming down her face. "It's too late. I've strayed too far. He won't take me back now."

Lucía scooted closer, kneeling beside Isabel and taking her trembling hands in hers. She wrote slowly, her eyes steady and filled with certainty: **"He never left you. He's waiting for you."**

Isabel stared at the words, her tears falling freely. "How can you believe that after everything?"

Lucía cupped Isabel's face in her hands, forcing her to meet her gaze. Her pen moved again: **"Because I see Him in you, even now."**

Isabel turned to her sister, her eyes brimming with uncertainty. Her voice broke as she asked, "What if I fail again? What if I go back and it's all too much?"

Lucía didn't hesitate. She set her notebook down and moved to sit beside Isabel, her movements slow and deliberate. Reaching out, she tucked a stray lock of hair behind Isabel's ear, her touch tender and grounding. Then she wrote: **"You don't have to carry this alone. He's waiting for you. So am I."**

The words pierced through Isabel's fragile defenses, and her tears fell freely. "It feels like my life is slipping away," she whispered. "Like everything I thought I was—everything I thought I could be—is just... gone. Was this all orchestrated by Him? Did He show me the path to Robert? Was it a test? A punishment?"

Lucía's gaze softened, and she reached for the notebook again. Her strokes were slow but deliberate: **"Sometimes we stumble. Sometimes we fall. But He doesn't leave us behind."**

Isabel stared at the words, her breath hitching. "So, you're saying... I chose this?"

Lucía nodded, then wrote: **"Yes. But choosing doesn't make you lose. It makes you human. And it brought you here."**

"Here?" Isabel's voice cracked, a mixture of disbelief and sorrow. "I don't even know where 'here' is anymore."

Lucía reached for Isabel's hand, holding it firmly. She wrote again, her strokes steady: **"Here is where you begin again."**

Isabel's tears spilled over as she leaned into Lucía's shoulder, her body trembling with the weight of her grief and longing. "Do you really think He'll take me back?"

Lucía didn't write this time. She simply wrapped her arms around Isabel, holding her as tightly as she could, her silence more profound than any words.

The sunlight shifted, casting soft patterns on the walls. Isabel felt the faintest flicker of hope, a fragile ember in the ashes of her doubts. She didn't speak again, but in her heart, a quiet voice whispered: **Take the first step. I'll catch you if you fall.**

10

The Road Back

The sun rose sluggishly, its light filtering through the thin curtains of the nearly empty apartment. Boxes were stacked neatly against the walls, and the suitcases by the door sat ready for the journey. The room felt hollow, stripped of its usual warmth, as though reflecting the weight of what was left unsaid between the two sisters.

Lucía stood by the window, her notebook open in her hands, her pen poised but unmoving. Her expression was serene, her gaze distant, but Isabel knew better. Beneath that calm exterior was an unwavering resolve that both comforted and unnerved her.

Isabel sat on the couch, staring at the packed suitcases. "This doesn't feel real," she murmured, breaking the silence. "It's like... everything we've been through is packed in those bags, waiting to follow us back."

Lucía turned toward her, her pen moving swiftly. She held the notebook up: **"Not everything. Just what matters."**

Isabel let out a hollow laugh, leaning back against the couch. "That's easy for you to say. You've been ready for this since the moment we left."

Lucía wrote again: **"Not true. I had to learn, too."**

"Learn what?" Isabel pressed, her voice sharper than she intended. "How to always know the right thing to say? How to make me feel like I'm failing without even trying?"

Lucía's expression didn't falter. Her pen moved deliberately across the page: **"How to trust."**

The words hit Isabel harder than she expected. She turned away, pretending to focus on the faint sounds of the city outside. "Well, you're better at it than I am."

Lucía crossed the room, placing the notebook gently on the table in front of Isabel. She tapped it once, then stepped away to continue tidying.

Isabel hesitated before picking it up. The page contained only one word: **"Ready?"**

She slammed the notebook shut, tossing it aside. "No. I'm not ready. I don't know if I'll ever be ready." Her voice cracked, betraying the frustration simmering beneath the surface.

Lucía paused her movements, her back still to Isabel. Then, without looking, she wrote another note and held it over her shoulder. **"You don't have to be ready. You just have to go."**

The bus station was bustling with noise and movement. Travelers hurried past with bags in tow, announcements cracked over the loudspeakers, and the scent of diesel mingled with the faint aroma of coffee from a nearby kiosk. Isabel clutched the strap of her bag tightly, her gaze darting nervously as they approached the platform.

Lucía remained close, her presence steady as always. She wrote a quick note and handed it to Isabel: **"Stay nearby. We'll leave together."**

"I'm not going anywhere," Isabel muttered, though her voice lacked conviction.

They boarded the bus in silence, finding seats near the window. As the vehicle rumbled to life, Isabel glanced out, watching the city shrink behind them. The further they traveled, the quieter the world seemed, until it was just the hum of the engine and the sound of her own thoughts.

At a small stop in the countryside, the bus pulled into a station. Passengers filed off for a brief rest, stretching their legs or seeking out refreshments. Isabel hesitated but finally stood, needing fresh air to clear her mind.

Lucía remained seated, her notebook resting on her lap. She watched Isabel with quiet curiosity as she got off the bus.

Isabel wandered to a nearby bench, where an older man sat alone, his hat pulled low over his face. He looked up as she approached, his eyes kind and filled with wisdom that seemed to reach beyond the moment.

"You look like someone carrying too much," he said, his voice warm but steady.

She blinked, surprised by his directness. "Excuse me?"

He gestured to the space beside him. "Sit. It helps to talk sometimes."

Isabel hesitated, then sat, her hands folded tightly in her lap. "I'm not sure what there is to say."

The man smiled faintly. "Start with the truth."

Isabel laughed bitterly. "The truth? That's complicated."

"All truths are," he said simply.

She glanced at him, her defenses cracking under his calm gaze. "I've made mistakes. Big ones. Ones I'm not sure I can come back from."

The man nodded slowly. "Mistakes don't define you. They refine you."

Isabel frowned, the words sinking in deeper than she wanted to admit. "What if I've strayed too far?"

"There's no such thing," the man replied. "Not with Him." He said pointing up to the sky.

Her breath caught. "You sound awfully certain."

"I've had my share of wandering," he said with a soft chuckle. "But the path always finds its way back to you, if you let it."

The bus horn blared, signaling it was time to leave. Isabel stood abruptly, her heart pounding. "Thank you," she said, her voice barely above a whisper.

The man tipped his hat. "Safe travels, child."

Back on the bus, Isabel dropped into her seat beside Lucía, her body heavy with exhaustion. The engine rumbled beneath them, its low vibration a constant, lulling rhythm. Yet, for Isabel, there was no peace in the sound—only the relentless churn of her thoughts.

She stared out the window as the scenery blurred past, her hands fidgeting in her lap. The stranger's words replayed in her mind, each one cutting deeper, peeling back layers she'd spent months building to protect herself. A single question rose unbidden, swelling like a wave she couldn't hold back.

"I don't know if I can stand in front of God again," she murmured, her voice barely audibles over the hum of the bus. The words were not meant for anyone, yet they hung in the air between her and Lucía like a confession.

Lucía glanced at her, her expression calm but searching. She reached for her notebook, the motion unhurried, and began to write with deliberate strokes.

When she finished, she turned the page toward Isabel. The words were simple, yet they carried a weight that stopped Isabel's breath: **"You already have."**

The color drained from Isabel's face. She stared at the words, her pulse quickening as the meaning began to unfold. Slowly, her gaze shifted to Lucía, whose calm expression revealed no surprise, no hesitation—only certainty.

"What do you mean?" Isabel asked, her voice trembling.

Lucía didn't answer. Instead, she nodded toward the window, her eyes urging Isabel to look back.

Isabel turned quickly, pressing her forehead to the glass as her eyes searched for the platform they'd just left. The bench where the old man had been sitting was empty, the space eerily still.

Her heart raced. "No... that's not possible," she whispered, her words breaking under the weight of realization.

The memory of the man's gaze, his words, his presence of it rushed back to her in a flood. Her hand flew to her mouth as tears welled in her eyes, spilling over before she could stop them.

"Lucía," she choked out, her voice thick with emotion. "Was that—was He—?"

Lucía didn't need to write this time. She simply reached over, taking Isabel's trembling hand in hers. Her grip was firm, grounding, as though to anchor Isabel in the truth that had just unraveled before her.

Isabel stared at her sister, the words she needed caught somewhere between her mind and her lips. Finally, she whispered, "Thank you, God," the words tumbling out in a prayer she hadn't meant to say aloud.

Lucía smiled faintly, the kind of smile that held no triumph, only understanding.

Isabel turned her gaze back out of the window, her chest rising and falling with shaky breaths. The bus began to pick up speed, carrying them further from the station and closer to their destination. But the echo of the stranger's words lingered, filling the space within her that had felt so hollow for so long.

The scenery outside grew softer as the light began to fade, the sky streaked with the warm hues of sunset. Isabel leaned her head against the window, her tears slowing as a quiet peace settled over her. She had spent so much time running, hiding, doubting. And now, for the first time in what felt like years, she was still.

Lucía's hand remained on hers, steady and unyielding. Isabel glanced at her sister; her voice steady but soft. "Do you think I'll ever feel worthy again?"

Lucía picked up her pen and wrote carefully: **"You're not called because you're worthy. You're made worthy because you're called."**

Isabel closed her eyes, letting the words sink deep into her soul. The bus rumbled on, carrying them closer to the place where everything began—and where everything would begin again.

11

The Final Light

The bells of the convent tolled softly as Lucía and Isabel passed through its gates, the sound reverberating in the stillness of the evening like a familiar hymn calling them home. The courtyard, untouched by time, seemed to embrace them with its quiet beauty—the worn stone paths, the gentle rustling of leaves, and the faint aroma of lavender from the garden.

The nuns lined the pathway, their hands folded in prayer, their smiles serene and welcoming. Their silence spoke volumes, carrying the weight of acceptance and love. It was as if the walls themselves breathed a collective sigh of relief, finally drawing back those who had been missing.

At the entrance stood Mother Superior, her tall, dignified figure bathed in the golden hues of the setting sun. Her presence commanded reverence, yet her eyes shone with warmth and kindness. She stepped forward, opening her arms as her gaze settled on the two sisters.

"Welcome home, my children," she said, her voice steady and soothing, carrying a weight of understanding that made Isabel's knees nearly buckle.

Lucía stepped forward first, her notebook clutched tightly in her hand. She opened it with care, her pen gliding across the page before she held it out for Mother Superior to read: **"We've come back."**

Mother Superior took Lucía's hand in both of hers, her grip gentle yet firm. She turned to Isabel, extending the same touch. "Yes," she said, her voice barely above a whisper. "You've come back. And your cell remains as you left it. It has waited for you, just as He has."

Isabel hesitated; her feet rooted to the ground as if the weight of the moment was too much to bear. Her suitcase felt heavier in her grasp, a physical reminder of all she carried—guilt, fear, and unspoken questions.

Mother Superior's gaze softened, and she stepped closer, placing a hand gently on Isabel's shoulder. "Come, my child," she said, her tone filled with reassurance. "This is not the place for burdens. This is the place for healing."

Isabel's lips trembled, but no words came. She nodded faintly, clutching the suitcase as if it might anchor her in the overwhelming sea of her emotions.

Lucía stepped closer, holding the notebook out once more, her writing deliberates and clear: **"We are ready to begin again."**

Mother Superior read the words and smiled, her expression filled with a quiet joy. She turned back to the gathered nuns, raising a hand in a gesture of blessing. "Let us welcome our sisters with open hearts," she said. "They have come back to the arms of grace."

The nuns bowed their heads, murmuring prayers of thanksgiving.

As they entered the main hall, the soft light of candles flickered along the walls, casting long, dancing shadows. Mother Superior walked ahead, her steps slow and deliberate, as if giving them time to absorb the familiarity of the place.

"Do you remember this hallway?" she asked, glancing over her shoulder at Isabel. "How often you ran through it as a novice, carrying books and always forgetting your veil?"

A faint, shaky smile tugged at Isabel's lips. "I remember," she whispered, her voice barely audible.

They continued in silence until they reached the door to their cell. Mother Superior stopped, her hand resting on the worn wooden handle. "This room has waited for you," she said, her voice tinged with emotion. "Not a single thing has been moved since you left. It is as it was, and it will be as it needs to be"

She pushed the door open, revealing the simple space within. Two narrow beds stood on opposite sides, their frames sturdy but unadorned. A small table held a candle and a well-worn Bible, its pages yellowed with time.

"Go," Mother Superior said, stepping aside to let them enter. "Settle down, rest, and pray. You are home again."

Lucía entered first, placing her suitcase carefully by the bed. Isabel lingered at the doorway, her eyes scanning the room as memories flooded back. Tears filled her eyes, blurring her vision, but she made no effort to stop them.

"You're safe here," Mother Superior added gently. "Whatever storms you've weathered, they end here. This is your refuge."

Isabel finally stepped inside, setting her suitcase down with trembling hands. She turned to Mother Superior, her voice breaking as she said, "Thank you."

Mother Superior placed a hand over Isabel's heart, her touch both firm and tender. "No need for thanks, my child. This is where you've always belonged."

As the door closed behind them, Lucía opened her notebook, writing quickly before showing it to Isabel: **"Rest. You are not alone anymore."**

Isabel sank onto the edge of her bed, her shoulders shaking as she wept quietly. Lucía sat beside her, wrapping an arm around her in silent support. The flicker of the candlelight illuminated their faces, casting their bond in warm, gentle light.

Outside, the bells tolled again, their sound carrying through the halls, signaling not just the end of a day but the beginning of something new.

A Gradual Decline

Days turned into weeks, and the rhythm of convent life embraced them like an old friend. But Isabel's strength began to falter. Her steps grew slower, her once-bright laughter now only a faint echo in the corridors.

Lucía watched over her sister with quiet vigilance, helping her dress, eat, and move about the convent. The other nuns noticed, their expressions softening with concern as they prayed for Isabel's healing.

One crisp evening, Mother Superior found Lucía outside the chapel, her notebook resting on her lap. She sat beside her, the silence between them filled with unspoken understanding.

"She is slipping," Mother Superior said softly.

Lucía nodded, her pen moving across the page: **"Her body is tired, but her soul is finding peace."**

Mother Superior closed her eyes, her lips moving in a silent prayer. "May He grant her the strength she needs, and may He grant us the grace to accept His will."

The Final Night

The call came in the dead of night. A young novice rapped softly at Mother Superior's door, her face pale. "It's Sister Isabel," she whispered. "She's worsening."

Mother Superior rose immediately, her robe trailing behind her as she hurried down the corridor. The air was heavy with the weight of unspoken fears.

When she entered Isabel's room, the nuns who had been tending to her stepped aside. "Go to the chapel and pray," Mother Superior instructed. "Lucía will stay with me."

Lucía stood by the bed, her notebook clutched to her chest. Isabel's face was pale, her breaths shallow, but her eyes fluttered open when she felt the presence of her sister and the Mother Superior.

"Mother," Isabel whispered, her voice frail, "I ask for forgiveness."

Mother Superior knelt beside Isabel's bed, taking her cold, trembling hand in hers. Isabel's lips quivered as she struggled to speak. Finally, her voice, barely more than a whisper, broke the silence.

"Mother... I've failed Him," she said, her words fractured by sobs. "I broke every vow, every promise. I betrayed everything I thought I was."

Mother Superior's brow furrowed, but her gaze remained tender. "Child, no one is beyond His love. No mistake you've made could ever separate you from His mercy."

Isabel's tears flowed freely. "You don't understand," she rasped, her voice shaking. "I gave myself to a man. I thought it was love, but it wasn't. It was... deception. I wanted so badly to feel seen, to feel... human. And now I feel like I've lost everything that made me His."

Mother Superior's grip on her hand tightened, her expression unwavering. "Isabel," she said firmly, "you are His now as much as you were the day you first knelt at His altar. The journey you've taken may have strayed, but it has brought you back to Him."

Isabel shook her head weakly, turning her face away. "How can He forgive me when I can't forgive myself?"

At that moment, Lucía stepped forward, her notebook open. She wrote slowly, her movements deliberate and held the page up for Isabel to read: **"Love does not need to be forgiven."**

Isabel's lips trembled as she read the words, and her sobs deepened. "How can you say that?" she whispered, her voice cracking.

Lucía stepped closer, her calm presence a balm against the storm of Isabel's anguish. She wrote again: **"He sent you to see the world. To feel its pain, its betrayal, its longing. So you would understand the depth of His love."**

Isabel's breath hitched as Lucía's words sank in. Mother Superior leaned forward, her voice soft but resolute. "You are loved, Isabel. Even in your darkest hour, you were never abandoned. His light has always been with you, waiting for you to turn back toward it."

Isabel met Mother Superior's gaze, her tears falling freely now. "Do you truly believe that?"

Mother Superior smiled, her own eyes glistening. "I don't just believe it, child. I know it. And deep down, so do you"

Lucía moved closer, placing the notebook gently in Isabel's lap. She wrote one last message, her strokes steady and clear: **"It's time to let go."**

Isabel's body trembled, her sobs breaking into uneven breaths. "Thank you," she whispered, her voice filled with a mixture of sorrow and gratitude.

Lucía reached out, her hand resting over Isabel's heart, her silent presence radiating strength. The candlelight in the room flickered once more, as if in agreement, before the quiet returned.

The light in the room shifted, soft and warm, as if the divine itself had entered. Lucía's figure seemed to glow, her presence radiant yet comforting. She leaned closer, her pen moving once more: **"It's time."**

Lucía extended her hand, her movements gentle but resolute. Isabel stared at it, her breathing uneven, her tears unending. "I'm afraid," she whispered.

For the first time, Lucía opened her mouth, her voice clear and melodic, filled with a power that seemed to reach beyond the walls of the convent. "Go to Him. He is waiting for you."

Isabel's trembling hand reached out, clasping Lucía's. A soft, golden light began to fill the room, growing brighter until it enveloped them entirely. Isabel stood; her steps steady as though her body had shed its frailty.

The light opened before them, a path that shimmered with an otherworldly beauty. Isabel turned to Lucía, her face filled with awe and peace. "Thank you," she said, her voice strong and certain.

Lucía smiled, her glow intensifying as she whispered, "He has always been waiting."

Isabel stepped into the light, her figure disappearing into its brilliance. And then, as suddenly as it had appeared, the light was gone.

The room fell silent once more, the glow replaced by darkness. Lucía turned back to face Mother Superior, who sat beside Isabel's lifeless body, her hands clasping Isabel's gently.

Tears streamed down Mother Superior's face as she looked at Lucía, her voice trembling. "She's gone."

Lucía knelt beside her, placing the notebook in Mother Superior's lap. Written there in her familiar handwriting were the words: **"She is home."**

Mother Superior's hands trembled as she read the words. She whispered a prayer, her voice breaking. "May she find eternal peace in His arms."

Lucía placed her hand over Mother Superior's, her presence steady and unyielding. Together, they remained by Isabel's side, the quiet room filled with the lingering warmth of grace.

As dawn broke over the convent, its golden light spilling through the arched windows, Lucía stood at the entrance to the chapel, her notebook cradled in her hands. The nuns moved quietly around her, their prayers and hymns filling the air with a serene harmony. She no longer felt like the silent observer she once was. She had become a quiet but undeniable force, her presence a balm to those who sought guidance, her words written with divine clarity offering solace to the lost.

Every soul that entered the convent seemed to find their way to her—broken hearts, trembling hands, and uncertain eyes. And though she never spoke, her words spoke louder than any voice. She had become what she was always meant to be: a vessel, a bridge, a reflection of God's unyielding love.

As she walked through the stone corridors, her notebook close to her chest, she paused before a single, flickering candle. Her hand brushed the flame gently, and for a moment, it seemed to burn brighter. She smiled faintly, her heart steady, her purpose clear. In the quiet of her soul, she prayed, her words now a whisper carried on the wind:

"Show me the next path, Lord. I will walk it."

The convent bells tolled, and Lucía turned toward the sound, her steps firm and resolute as she moved forward into the light, ready to guide another soul home.

Acknowledments

To those who find light even in the darkest moments, this story is for you.

Writing *Written in Light* has been a journey into the soul—a discovery of words and the truths that live between them. It has reminded me that light is not something we chase; it is something we carry, waiting for the right moment to shine.

To my readers: thank you for opening your hearts to this story. You are the light bearers, the seekers of hope, and the proof that words can spark change. Your willingness to embrace this journey gives it life beyond the page.

To my wife, who has been my unwavering companion and my brightest star—thank you for your love, patience, and belief in me, even when I doubted myself. To my children and grandchildren, you are my living legacy, the light I see in every sunrise, and the joy that reminds me why we share our stories.

Finally, to the divine spirit that flows through us all, thank you for the whispers of inspiration, the lessons found in both struggle and triumph and the reminder that shadows only exist to amplify the brilliance of the light.

This story is not just mine—it's ours. It reflects our trials, courage, and the boundless capacity of the human spirit to overcome.

With profound gratitude,

Antonio Garrido Caballero